ROUTLEDGE LIBRARY EDITIONS:
COLD WAR SECURITY STUDIES

Volume 17

CONVENTIONAL WARFARE IN THE NUCLEAR AGE

CONVENTIONAL WARFARE IN THE NUCLEAR AGE

OTTO HEILBRUNN

LONDON AND NEW YORK

First published in 1965 by George Allen & Unwin Ltd

This edition first published in 2021
by Routledge
2 Park Square, Milton Park, Abingdon, Oxon OX14 4RN

and by Routledge
605 Third Avenue, New York, NY 10017

Routledge is an imprint of the Taylor & Francis Group, an informa business

© 1965 George Allen & Unwin Ltd

All rights reserved. No part of this book may be reprinted or reproduced or utilised in any form or by any electronic, mechanical, or other means, now known or hereafter invented, including photocopying and recording, or in any information storage or retrieval system, without permission in writing from the publishers.

Trademark notice: Product or corporate names may be trademarks or registered trademarks, and are used only for identification and explanation without intent to infringe.

British Library Cataloguing in Publication Data
A catalogue record for this book is available from the British Library

ISBN 13: 978-0-367-56630-2 (Set)
ISBN 13: 978-1-00-312438-2 (Set) (ebk)
ISBN 13: 978-0-367-55734-8 (Volume 17) (hbk)
ISBN 13: 978-1-00-309491-3 (Volume 17) (ebk)

Publisher's Note
The publisher has gone to great lengths to ensure the quality of this reprint but points out that some imperfections in the original copies may be apparent.

Disclaimer
The publisher has made every effort to trace copyright holders and would welcome correspondence from those they have been unable to trace.

CONVENTIONAL WARFARE IN THE NUCLEAR AGE

OTTO HEILBRUNN

London
GEORGE ALLEN & UNWIN LTD
RUSKIN HOUSE · MUSEUM STREET

FIRST PUBLISHED IN 1965
*This book is copyright under the Berne Convention.
Apart from any fair dealing for the purpose of private
study, research, criticism or review, as permitted under
the Copyright Act, 1956, no portion may be reproduced
by any process without written permission. Inquiries
should be made to the publishers*

© *George Allen & Unwin Ltd., 1965*

PRINTED IN GREAT BRITAIN
in 11 point Baskerville type
BY C. TINLING AND COMPANY
LIVERPOOL, LONDON AND PRESCOT

ACKNOWLEDGEMENTS

Most of the research for this book was done at the Royal United Service Institution. I am greatly indebted to its Director, Brigadier John Stephenson, OBE, for the constant encouragement I have received from him, including the privilege of working in the Institution's stimulating atmosphere which he has done so much to create.

I am also grateful to my American Publishers, Frederick A. Praeger Inc., for permission to quote from *Military Strategy—Soviet Doctrine and Concepts*, edited by Marshal Sokolovsky. My indebtedness to other published works is acknowledged in the text, and I record my obligation to Major-General Lancelot E. C. M. Perowne, CB, CBE, for allowing me to use his hitherto unpublished Report on the Operations of the 23rd British Infantry Brigade, Naga Hills, April—July 1944.

The responsibility for the contents of the book is of course entirely mine.

CONTENTS

INTRODUCTION   page 11

PART I: THE INFLUENCE OF NUCLEAR DOCTRINE ON CONVENTIONAL WARFARE

1. THE SETTING FOR CONVENTIONAL WARFARE   17

   The Nuclear Deterrent as its own Counter-Deterrent—Increased Likelihood of Limited War—Tactical Nuclear Weapons are no Substitute for Conventional Capability—NATO's Need of Conventional Forces—The Present State of the NATO Debate.

2. THE NEW PATTERN OF CONVENTIONAL WARFARE   28

   The Advantages of the Attacker: Surprise, Choice of Weapons and Depth of Operations (Rear Warfare)—Past Aims of Rear Warfare—The New Possibilities: Air Transport of Armoured and Motorized Forces—The Significance of the New Capabilities—The Soviet Doctrine and Western Concepts on Rear Attack in the Combat Zone.

3. DEPLOYMENT IN NUCLEAR WAR   38

   Is Nuclear Deployment required in Conventional War?—The Doctrines of Nuclear Land Warfare Operations: The Rejection of the Static Defence Concept; Nuclear Targets: Key Areas or Troops? The Significance of Troop Concentration and Dispersion; Occupation or Control of Territory? Interchange between Offensive and Defensive Actions; The Depth of the Battlefield; Supply Problems; Fire-power and Movement; Target Acquisition and Air Superiority—Nuclear Battle Tactics—Nuclear Deployment—Grand Tactics.

PART II: A CONCEPT FOR CONVENTIONAL WARFARE

4. DEPLOYMENT FOR CONVENTIONAL WAR   63

   Is Nuclear Deployment Suitable for Conventional War?—The Continuous Front in World War I—Blitzkrieg, Area and Mobile Defence in World War II—The Defence Advantages on the Conventional Battlefield: The Attacker's Need of Numerical Superiority over the Defence—The Drawbacks of Nuclear Deployment in Conventional War: The Influence of Mobile Defence, Dispersal of Forces and Extension of Battlefield on the required Ratio of Forces; The Defender's Need for numerical Near-Parity—The Disadvantages of Dual Deployment—Can the Defence Switch from Conventional to Nuclear Deployment?—The Attacker's Preference for Nuclear Deployment—The Defence Requirements for Conventional War: Nuclear Deployment and Near-Parity of Forces.

CONTENTS

5. THE DISTRIBUTION OF TROOPS OVER THE FRONT AND REAR ... 89

The Reasons for Upgrading Rear Warfare—The Combination of Frontal Defence with Rear Attack—General Wingate's Concept of Rear-Fighting—Harassing Missions in the Enemy Rear: Co-ordination in Strategy, Campaigns and Battles—Combat Missions in the Enemy Rear: Strategic and Tactical Employment of Troops—The Power of Survival in the Enemy Far Rear: Partisans and Chindits—The Stronghold Concept—Large-scale Penetration by Ground Approach in Europe—The Aims of Combat Forces in the Near Rear: Pulling Back the Enemy Front. The Tactics: Isolation of the Battlefield and Co-operation in Envelopment—The Concept of Concentric Dispersion—Assistance by Special Forces and Partisans to the Rear Combat Forces—German Aptitude for Partisan Operations—The Security of our own Rear: NATO Troops and Territorial Defence Units—Distribution Key for Front and Rear Troops.

6. TECHNICAL PROBLEMS OF CONVENTIONAL WARFARE ... 113

The Structure for Nuclear War—Its Suitability for Conventional War—Tanks Are Not Obsolete—The Need for Armoured Infantry—Artillery Shortages—Air Superiority—Army Aviation—The Future Role of Airborne Troops—Are Dual Purpose Weapons Necessary?—Bacteriological and Chemical Warfare—Communications—Training for Nuclear and Conventional War—The Short-comings of the Supply Service.

7. THE SWITCH FROM CONVENTIONAL TO NUCLEAR WAR ... 129

Reasons of the Defence for a Switch—Reasons of the Attacker for a Switch—The Advantages and Disadvantages for Defender and Attacker.

PART III: CONCLUSIONS

8. AN ASSESSMENT OF THE DEBATE ... 139

APPENDIX: OPERATIONS OF THE 23RD BRITISH INFANTRY BRIGADE, NAGA HILLS, APRIL—JULY 1944 ... 145

BIBLIOGRAPHY ... 154

INDEX ... 161

INTRODUCTION

THE Western Alliance is at present able to deter a nuclear attack by its retaliatory, nuclear, capability. The West must also be able to discourage conventional aggression by conventional capability and, if this fails, to meet conventional attack with conventional defence; only if the attack cannot otherwise be repelled should the West resort to nuclear weapons.

This line of thought is not everywhere accepted within the Western Alliance but there is growing support, in theory at least if not in practice, for the view that NATO needs stronger conventional forces in order to have the option of nuclear or conventional defence in face of a conventional attack. The NATO Council decided at its Paris meeting in December 1960 that 'there must be a proper balance in the forces of the Alliance of nuclear and conventional strength to provide the required flexibility', and in May 1963 it was agreed at the NATO Ministerial Council meeting in Ottawa to establish 'a more satisfactory balance' between nuclear and conventional forces.

Conventional war under nuclear threat will be different from the last war and the last war but one. Must the aims of strategy and grand tactics be modified? Is it possible and indeed necessary, as is generally supposed, to deploy the conventional defence as if it were fighting in a nuclear war? Can the defence be deployed in such a way as to be able to meet both a nuclear and a conventional attack? Must the attacker always concentrate or can he achieve his aim by other means? When has the defence no longer an advantage over the attacker and what ought to be regarded as the required ratio of strength between the two sides? Is the structure of ground forces, organized for fighting a nuclear war, suitable for conventional warfare? What role can tanks and airborne forces play in the future? When is the stage reached at which one side can be expected to use nuclear weapons and what can it hope to gain therefrom at that stage? Is it possible to switch on the battlefield from conventional to nuclear war?

There is one further question of particular importance: what significance will warfare in the enemy's rear have in the future? Is it possible, by thus shifting the weight of attack as much as possible from the front to the rear, to avoid concentration for the attack without markedly diminishing its impetus?

These, then, are some of the questions discussed in this book. Strategic thinking has for so long been dominated by the planners' insistence that any war in western Europe must be nuclear, that discussion of conventional warfare was almost relegated to the realm of science fiction. The new look in NATO's policy makes it appear timely to re-examine the doctrine and investigate the problems of a future conventional war in Europe further than has hitherto been done.

It is true, of course, that published statements on Soviet doctrine all stress that a war between nuclear powers cannot be conventional but is bound to become nuclear. It must not be overlooked, though, that the Soviets cannot possibly have any interest in asserting the contrary and thereby accelerating the emergence of stronger NATO conventional forces. What is more, the Soviets have a large Army trained for nuclear *and* conventional war, and it is difficult to envisage any contingency in which this could be required for conventional duties anywhere but in Europe.[1] Hence Soviet pronouncements must not deter the Western Alliance from formulating a conventional strategy and providing the means to enforce it.

According to American Intelligence estimates prior to about the middle of 1963, Soviet Russia had 175 active divisions. However, in a policy speech made on November 18, 1963, before the Economic Club in New York the US Defence Secretary, Mr Robert McNamara, announced that the Soviet strength was in fact less than half that number.[2] The NATO strength in Central Europe is at present about 23 and a half divisions. The NATO target, before and after the drastic revision of the Intelligence estimates, was and presumably still is 30 divisions.

The Soviets have 20 divisions in East Germany, three in Hungary and two in Poland, a total of 25 divisions. They can use 60 divisions of the other Warsaw Pact countries to neutralize any threat from the NATO flanks, and build up their forward strength to 65 Soviet divisions in the first month and to about

---

[1] A hot war between Soviet Russia and China is unlikely but should it break out it must become nuclear at once, firstly because China's enormous numerical superiority would give Soviet Russia no other choice, and secondly because she would want to bring such a war to a rapid end in order not to denude her western frontier of troops for any length of time.

[2] Cf. *The Times* (London), November 19, 1963.

INTRODUCTION

100 in the second month of mobilization, while NATO could count on only 12 reserve divisions or a total of about 35 divisions in the first month.[1]

However, in view of the different strengths of NATO and Warsaw Pact divisions, a comparison by numbers of divisions is somewhat misleading. As Mr McNamara has pointed out, if the NATO Alliance were to reorganize along Soviet lines it could display a far greater number of divisions. According to his statement NATO's ground forces in Europe total 2,200,000 men, as against a Warsaw Pact total of about 3 million. In Central Europe the numerical advantage is at present with NATO. 'In Central Europe', Mr McNamara has said, 'NATO has more men, and more combat troops, on the ground than does the bloc. It has more men on the ground in west Germany than the bloc does in east Germany', and Mr Neville Brown estimates the present NATO troop strength in the central area at 975,000 men as against 665,000 men of the Warsaw Pact forces.[2]

But the picture would be different in case of an emergency. It is held that the Soviets could reinforce, before an outbreak, their 25 divisions to 40 divisions without necessarily attracting the attention of the West. The Red Army has also 10 airborne divisions available. Furthermore, the Warsaw bloc can increase its troop strength much faster than the NATO Alliance. The numerical advantage of the Warsaw bloc would then be considerable.

In December 1963, the Soviet Union announced a 4.3 per cent cut in defence spending. While the consequence of this announcement cannot yet be assessed in concrete terms, it could signify an eight per cent reduction of the conventional forces, and both sides may in future make further changes in troop strength. As long as the forces of both sides are about equal in numbers, NATO does not require more active divisions but it does need larger and more quickly available combat-ready reserves, more and better equipment, and improved administrative support. It is mainly in that sense that we speak here of NATO's need of stronger conventional forces and greater conventional strength.

---

[1] In Alastair Buchan and Philip Windsor, *Arms and Stability in Europe* (London and New York, 1963), p. 21.
[2] Neville Brown, 'The Armies in Central Europe', *The Royal United Service Institution Journal*, November 1963, Vol. CVIII, No. 632, p. 348.

INTRODUCTION

The conclusions reached in this study are of a general nature and are not affected by the respective number of armed forces at any given time. But the book is not merely an academic study. It is written in relation to an actual NATO war in which NATO appears in the role of the defender.

PART I

THE INFLUENCE OF NUCLEAR DOCTRINE ON CONVENTIONAL WARFARE

CHAPTER 1

THE SETTING FOR CONVENTIONAL WARFARE

NUCLEAR war has been described as unacceptable and unthinkable but it has become so only very recently. As long as the United States had nuclear hegemony or supremacy, Soviet military doctrine professed not to be disturbed by the advent of the new weapon; no single weapon could win a war; decisive were the permanently operating factors in which the Soviet Union was supreme. As for the West, it intended to use these weapons if it were attacked; any Soviet attack in western Europe would automatically provoke nuclear retaliation. In doctrine at least nuclear war was presented by both sides as acceptable.

When, however, the Soviet Union managed to establish nuclear parity with the United States, the nuclear deterrent, previously thought of by the West as deterring an enemy, also became its own counter-deterrent: because either of the great nuclear powers is at present able to survive a nuclear attack upon itself and mount a devastating nuclear counter-attack, both must fear to use the weapon first.[1] That is unless one side succeeds at some future date in establishing overwhelming nuclear superiority, be it offensive by acquiring warfare-in-space capability, or defensive by developing an effective anti-missile missile. The attacker in either case need not necessarily be the superior side; the weaker opponent might wish to get in a preventive or pre-emptive first blow in order to wipe out as much as possible of the enemy's nuclear capability and thus restore the balance. The counter-deterrent also ceases to be effective if one side has almost lost the—conventional—war and uses the *Wunderwaffe* in a final desperate attempt to turn the scales.

Nuclear war may, of course, break out for other reasons. A commander in the field may decide to retrieve the local situ-

---

[1] For a closely reasoned argument that this fear is not always a guarantee against the outbreak of a nuclear war, cf., however, John Strachey, MP, *On the Prevention of War* (London, 1962; New York, 1963), pp. 50 ff.

ation in a hitherto conventional engagement by using so-called battlefield nuclear weapons. It requires a supreme act of faith to believe that nuclear exchange is a tit for tat. The enemy's nuclear reply may be directed not against the battle zone but against the far rear. It might still be tactical in a sense—and 'tactical' has many senses in the context of nuclear war—but explode over major rail junctions or airfields near cities.[1] Since the enemy has now hit large towns or cities, the field is wide open for further escalation and unlimited nuclear war. Indeed, as Mr Thorneycroft, the British Minister of Defence, stated in the House of Commons on July 3, 1963, 'the use of so-called tactical weapons must pose very grave risks of escalation'.[2]

The champions of the tactical nuclear weapon claim that its presence in the NATO arsenal prevents an enemy from launching even a limited conventional attack because he must fear this possible spiralling effect. But one can argue with equal conviction and more justification that tactical nuclear weapons lack credibility because an enemy will not credit his opponent with the folly of initiating a tactical nuclear exchange and unleashing unlimited nuclear war because he has been driven out of a railway junction. If the railway junction is not worth it, is the lost river position, the city, the county?

But further factors are bound to enter into the enemy's calculation: an Allied, say non-German, commander may order an initial tactical nuclear strike on German soil but would a Ger-

[1] The British Minister of Defence defined (in the House of Commons on April 3, 1963) a weapon as tactical if it is directed at a tactical target. In this view, it appears, even the largest nuclear devices could on occasion be regarded as tactical, and in the NATO area in Europe hardly a strategic target would escape destruction if the major tactical targets (troops, their supply and transport facilities, air bases, seaports and infrastructure) were subjected to nuclear attack with large devices. Cf. also Robert Endicott Osgood, *Limited War: The Challenge to American Strategy* (Chicago, 1957), pp. 254 ff.

The above is probably the first official British definition of a tactical nuclear weapon; the United States does not seem to have formulated one. A plea for distinction between tactical and strategic weapons is contained in *On Limiting Atomic War*, published by the Royal Institute of International Affairs (London, 1956). On the relation between tactical and limited strategic nuclear war, cf. Thornton Read, 'Limited Strategic War and Tactical Nuclear War', in Klaus Knorr and Thornton Read, *Limited Strategic War* (London and New York, 1962), pp. 67 ff.

[2] The other possibilities of an outbreak of nuclear war arise from mistake, miscalculation, or by way of escalation from a conventional conflict. Herman Kahn, *Thinking about the Unthinkable* (London and New York, 1962), pp. 40 ff., differentiates between inadvertent war, war as a result of miscalculation, calculated war, and catalytic war.

man commander do so? Would an American or British officer use, or ask permission to use, tactical weapons in defence of a small ally and court the risk of retaliation against his own country, especially if it has been drawn into the war against its will? A weapon is credible when the enemy knows that it will be used in certain circumstances but it has lost its aura of credibility when he starts considering the importance of an objective and the nationality of a commander in assessing the chances for or against its use.

Above all, the NATO threat to use tactical nuclear weapons could be credible only if the—initial—use of weapons of this category made sense. The formerly predominant Western idea that large conventional forces were not required because small ground forces equipped with tactical nuclear weapons could contain a strong conventional attack by the East was based on the assumption that the opponent would have to concentrate for the attack and thus offer a good nuclear target. This concept became outmoded when the East also equipped its forces with tactical nuclear weapons. The attacker, it is true, may no longer be able to concentrate large forces for an offensive—unless he takes a possibly miscalculated risk—but large concentrations are not necessarily required any more for an attack, since the defence can no longer concentrate without risk either. If the defence is not concentrated, the attacker can more easily infiltrate and reach the comparative safety of the defender's rear which the latter is unlikely to subject to nuclear bombardment because he would cut off his own supply lines and retreat routes. There is also still some scope, to say the least, for operations of the attacker in the rear of the defence; they make it possible to thin out the attacker's front even more.

It has also been said that the defence, by laying waste large areas with atomic bursts, could always force the attacker to concentrate at selected places and thus gain a decisive advantage. But this argument is no longer valid either since the attacker can now do likewise.

If fewer troops are required at any given time to man the defences, more are needed over a period to replace the greater number of casualties expected in a nuclear war. Furthermore, one must not lose sight of the fact that the war will possibly be fought on NATO soil, and the NATO defence will be more reluctant than the attacker to squander nuclear devices. What the individual strikes of the attacker may lack in effectiveness, he can easily make up by the number of strikes. If there is an advantage in a tactical nuclear exchange on NATO soil it is unlikely to be with the West. It seems bound, in fact, to suffer more. As Professor P. M. S. Blackett points out, the Western military effort must be supplied through a few ports and 'these would, on almost any set of rules for limited war, be allowed as targets for tactical nuclear weapons';[1] the East is not equally vulnerable.[2] At any rate, even if the nuclear exchange remained on the tactical level, the West would risk the extinction of large parts of Allied country.

In short, the presence of tactical nuclear weapons will not necessarily deter an enemy from launching a conventional attack, he cannot be expected to believe that the West will engage in what Colonel Gwynne Jones so rightly called 'this totally unreal form of warfare',[3] nor will tactical nuclear weapons make good the West's numerical inferiority in conventional reserves.[4]

NATO troops must have battlefield nuclear weapons because the East has them, not because they are deemed to be credible. Credible are in fact only the will of the victim of a nuclear—or an overwhelming conventional—attack to retaliate with nuclear

[1] In *Studies of War, Nuclear and Conventional* (Edinburgh and London, 1962), p. 61.
[2] In Lt.-General Sir John G. Cowley, 'Future Trends in Warfare', Lecture reprinted in *Royal United Service Institution Journal* (in future referred to as *RUSIJ*) February 1960, Vol. CV, No. 617, p. 8.
[3] Lt.-Colonel Alun Gwynne Jones, Defence Correspondent of *The Times* (London), 'Modern Strategic Concepts', Lecture reprinted in *RUSIJ*, February 1963, Vol. CVIII, No. 629, p. 9.
[4] Cf. for further arguments in this respect, Captain B. H. Liddell Hart, *Deterrent or Defence* (London and New York, 1960), pp. 78 ff., and 'Small Atomics— A Big Problem', *Marine Corps Gazette*, December 1959, Vol. 43, No. 12, p. 12; P. M. S. Blackett, op. cit., pp. 82 ff.; Alastair Buchan, *NATO in the 1960's* (London and New York, 1960), p. 86; Strachey, op. cit., p. 93; Roger Hilsman, 'NATO: The Developing Strategic Context', in Klaus Knorr (ed.), *NATO and American Security* (Princeton, 1959), p. 32; Malcolm W. Hoag, 'The Place of Limited War in NATO Strategy', also in Knorr, op. cit., p. 119; Roger Hilsman, 'Strategic Doctrines for Nuclear War', in William W. Kaufman (ed.), *Military Policy and National Security* (London and Princeton, 1956), p. 72. Cf. also William W. Kaufman, 'Force and Foreign Policy', ibid., p. 237; Lt.-Colonel F. O. Miksche, *The Failure of Atomic Strategy* (London and New York, 1959), p. 164; Helmut Schmidt, *Defence or Retaliation* (London and New York, 1962), p. 95; General Pickert, 'The Value of Numbers in the Nuclear Age', first published in *Revue Militaire Générale*, February 1961, p. 204; and in *Survival*, September/October 1961, Vol. 3, No. 5, pp. 229 ff.; Morton H. Halperin, *Limited War in the Nuclear Age* (London and New York, 1963), pp. 65 ff.

weapons, and his capability to do so. But as first strike weapons the nuclear devices, whether they are tactical or strategic, have otherwise lost much of their credibility because they fire *and* backfire with equal certainty.

'When both sides have nuclear sufficiency', Field Marshal Lord Montgomery has pointed out, 'the deterrent will merely serve to deter each side from using it as a weapon'.[1] That is, of course, unless one side attains nuclear supremacy. Until then, however, nuclear war is less probable. But the nuclear deterrent will not deter every type of war. A deterrent that is capable of preventing all-out war, does not necessarily prevent limited war. In fact, as General Hackett has indicated, it may invite it: 'One thing seems to be almost certain. If nuclear general war becomes less likely lesser forms of warfare become more'.[2] The back-fire effect of his own nuclear weapons could tempt an aggressor into conventional war if war he wants. And the defence has apparently no choice but to fight the war on conventional lines as long as possible because its nuclear weapons also backfire. The aggressor's objectives may be outside Europe but they need not be. NATO must therefore strengthen its conventional capability.

Two sets of objections have been raised against this line of argument:

1. A considerable body of opinion, especially on the European Continent, still insists that conventional and nuclear war can only be prevented by the threat of massive retaliation. The presence of strong conventional NATO forces or their conventional deployment could in this view only detract from the credibility of the deterrent.

---

[1] Field Marshal Viscount Montgomery, 'The Present State of the Game in the Contest Between East and West, and the Future Outlook', *RUSIJ*, November 1958, Vol. CIII, No. 612, p. 479. The Field Marshal spoke in the context of a minor Soviet aggression.

[2] Lt.-General Sir John W. Hackett in his Foreword to Otto Heilbrunn, *Warfare in the Enemy's Rear* (London 1963), p. 11. Cf. also Liddell Hart, *Deterrent or Defence*, p. 23: 'To the extent that the H-bomb reduces the likelihood of full-scale war, it *increases* the possibilities of limited war pursued by widespread local aggression.' Similarly the same author in 'Guerrilla War: Factors and Reflections', *Marine Corps Gazette*, December 1962, Vol. 46, No. 12, p. 22. Also Lt.-Colonel F. O. Miksche, op. cit., p. 170; Robert Endicott Osgood, op. cit., p. 5; Marshal of the RAF Sir John Slessor, *The Great Deterrent* (London, 1957), p. 193; Henry A. Kissinger, *Nuclear Weapons and Foreign Policy* (New York, 1957), pp. 96 and 126; and Raymond L. Garthoff, *Soviet Strategy in the Nuclear Age* (London 1958 and New York, Revised Edition, 1962), p. 114. Against this argument is General Pierre Gallois, *Stratégie de l'âge nucléaire* (Paris, 1960).

This view overlooks that the credibility of the nuclear devices as first-strike weapons is already discredited[1] and the argument is therefore unrealistic. Furthermore, the Allies cannot convince a potential aggressor that their unequivocal response to any conventional attack will be an unlimited nuclear counter-attack while they make strenuous efforts to agree among themselves on a system of joint control of the nuclear arm. Control includes, after all, the right to veto its use.[2]

It is surely wrong for NATO to 'stake the national substance on every dispute'[3] and treat every attack 'initially as a major crisis for lack of appropriate limited means of handling it'[4] or, alternatively, to incur 'a paralysis of decision which a resourceful adversary will exploit to the utmost'.[5] Indeed, as long as the West has insufficient conventional strength, it runs the risk 'of being forced by diplomatic blackmail into having to make the impossible choice of accepting as a *fait accompli* the occupation of some part of NATO territory or of starting a nuclear war'.[6]

Those who are opposed to the build-up of NATO's conventional capability overlook one factor of vital importance: NATO must never allow itself to be manoeuvred into a position where it has to make this 'impossible choice' because it might disrupt and virtually terminate the Alliance. Such an event would be catastrophic at any time; it might result in total surrender of Western Europe in critical times.

The deterrent is no more credible to an enemy than it is to us. It is credible, to friend and foe alike, if and when the use of

[1] Cf. also Lt.-Colonel Alun Gwynne Jones, op. cit., p. 5: 'As the nuclear arm is already only credible as a defence against nuclear attack, it is hard to see exactly what this [alleged erosion of the credibility] means.'

[2] On the question whether agreed political directives have been issued to the Supreme Allied Commander Europe for authorizing the initial tactical use of nuclear weapons, cf. F. W. Mulley, MP, *The Politics of Western Defence* (London and New York 1962), p. 108.

[3] Kissinger, op. cit., p. 285.

[4] Buchan, op. cit., p. 32. Cf. also Professor Michael Howard *Disengagement in Europe* (London and New York 1958), p. 47.

[5] Osgood, op. cit., p. 262.

[6] Mulley, op. cit., p. 14. Similarly Denis Healey, MP, House of Commons Debate, March 1, 1955, *Hansard*, col. 1935 f.; Strachey, op. cit., pp. 70 and 87 ff.; Miksche, op. cit., p. 119. He concludes that 'a power which relies too one-sidedly on atomic weapons becomes a very dangerous and at the same time politically a very unreliable ally'. But the same holds good for a NATO member faced with the choice between conciliation with the Soviets or nuclear destruction, as Osgood, op. cit., p. 262, points out. Cf. also ibid., pp. 237 and 261. Also Schmidt, op. cit., p. 18, and Alain C. Enthoven, 'American Deterrent Policy', address reprinted in *Survival*, May/June 1963, Vol. 5, No. 3, p. 96.

nuclear weapons is appropriate. It undermines the credibility to insist that we will use them on any and every occasion. This insistence increases the danger of war because it tempts an enemy to find out how much he can get away with; what is worse, the lack of sufficient conventional strength makes it feasible for him to promote and exploit the 'contradictions' within the Alliance to the point of splitting it.

It must therefore be recognized that 'the important thing is not to convince an aggressor that we will use nuclear weapons. The important thing is to convince him that we will use whatever force that is necessary to preserve our freedom',[1] and that force must be conventional in the appropriate cases.

2. Another school of thought believes that NATO does not require conventional capabilities since any conventional contest in Europe must by necessity become nuclear, because the losing side will either use nuclear weapons rather than accept defeat, or throw in so many reserves that the opponent, unable to match the raised level of attack, will resort to nuclear weapons. If, then, the war must become nuclear anyway, it is argued, why not reply at the outset with the threat of nuclear retaliation and retaliate?[2] The answer, it appears, is this: if the West is confronted with a massive conventional attack, nuclear weapons will be used in response. The problem therefore arises only if the conventional aggression is on a smaller scale. This can be contained by the West, without resort to nuclear weapons, if its conventional capability is raised. The attacker may disclose his intentions to the other side only in the course of hostilities. He may try a conventional *Blitzkrieg* with limited aims. In that case he is unlikely to provoke nuclear war or resort to nuclear weapons himself if a conventional defence manages to contain him; there is a very good chance indeed that he will withdraw and bring hostilities to an end. The defence would be reckless if it turned the conflict at once into a nuclear war instead of awaiting developments and fighting a conventional war in the meanwhile.[3]

---

[1] Enthoven, loc. cit. Also against the above views is Rear Admiral Sir Anthony Buzzard, 'Limited War Capability' *The Hawk, The Journal of the Royal Air Force Staff Colleges*, No. 24, December 1962, pp. 15 ff.

[2] Cf. for the statement of this theory Klaus Knorr, 'Aspects of NATO Strategy: A Conference Report', in op. cit., p. 324.

[3] Also against the above school of thought is Henry A. Kissinger, *The Necessity for Choice* (London, 1960; New York, 1961), p. 60.

One cannot therefore escape the conclusion that NATO's salvation lies in strengthening its conventional capability so as to be able to meet a conventional attack with conventional means, as far as possible and as long as possible.[1] The United States has adopted this position in 1961; President Kennedy stated in his special message to Congress on the defence budget (March 28, 1961) that 'in the event of a major aggression which cannot be repulsed by conventional forces, we must be prepared to take whatever action with whatever means are appropriate'.[2] Minor acts of aggression will therefore be answered with conventional forces; conventional aggression on a major scale will also be answered with conventional means, at least in the initial stage, if possible and, if it is not or if the attack is massive, nuclear weapons will be used.

However, on the European Continent it is widely held that a future conventional war will be almost as destructive as nuclear war and the view still prevails, as we have noted before, that only the unlimited threat of massive retaliation can avoid the outbreak of either, and that nuclear weapons must at once be used if the deterrent fails.

The British position comes closer to the European than the American concept. On June 1, 1961, the then British Defence Minister, addressing the Assembly of the Western European Union, went on record to say that NATO should not have such massive conventional forces as could hope to deal with any conventional attack, because such a policy would only indicate lack of courage to use the nuclear weapon under any circumstances. On the other hand the Alliance must not overdepend on nuclear weapons. 'Between these two extremes', he concluded, 'we must strike a balance on what the Alliance can afford without waste of resources.'

The dividing line was therefore somewhere between massive and minor attack, and it seemed at one time that the British had fully accepted the American view. At the Nassau Conference of December 21, 1962, the functions hitherto assigned to nuclear

---

[1] Cf. John Strachey, op. cit., p. 71: 'Woe betide the alliance which neglects it [the conventional capability], for it will sooner or later find itself outclassed at the conventional level, and deterred by the consequences to itself of going up to the next level.'

[2] This policy was foreshadowed in General Norstad's speeches to the Atlantic Congress in London (June 1959) and to NATO parliamentarians in Paris (June 1960).

and conventional defence were reversed and the latter up-graded in the process: while NATO had previously described its nuclear capability as its sword and its ground forces as the shield, the American President and the British Prime Minister agreed at Nassau to consider the nuclear devices as the shield and the ground forces as the sword; 'in addition to having a nuclear shield', the Communiqué stated, 'it is important to have a non-nuclear sword'.

It was in the circumstances not surprising that 'radical changes in BAOR strategy' were subsequently announced, especially that the emphasis in tactics and training would in future be on the non-nuclear phase of the defensive battle.[1] But it soon became clear that the views of British and American politicians on the scope for conventional warfare were far apart. These differences were not about force goals—they had been agreed—but about the duration of a conventional war and the consequent amount of supplies required. Prior to the NATO Council meeting in Ottawa on May 22, 1963, it became known that the Americans insisted on ninety days' stocks for troops in Europe while the British considered thirty days' supplies adequate.[2] The British position was restated by the Defence Minister in a speech in the House of Commons on July 3, 1963, when he said that it was neither possible nor seriously contemplated that conventional forces could be made available on a scale capable of fighting a prolonged conventional war. It therefore appears that in the British view even a smaller-scale attack will be answered with nuclear weapons if it cannot be quickly repelled; the Americans want to fight conventionally longer than the British. But it is also clear from the American pressure for larger conventional forces that the Americans want to raise the nuclear threshold higher than the British, that is to fight conventionally against stronger conventional attacks than the British envisage to do. While it was agreed by all in Ottawa that a more satisfactory balance between nuclear and conventional forces should be established, it is probably still true to say that the British 'expect to use tactical nuclear weapons in almost any contingency'.[3]

[1] Cf. 'Training for Non-nuclear Warfare', article by the Defence Correspondent, *The Times* (London), May 6, 1963.
[2] Cf. *The Times* (London), May 11, 1963.
[3] F. W. Mulley, MP, 'Europe and the Mediterranean', Lecture reprinted in *RUSIJ*, May 1963, Vol. CVIII, No. 630, p. 125.

CONVENTIONAL WARFARE IN THE NUCLEAR AGE

When NATO first formulated its strategic concept in February 1952, it relied heavily in its planning on conventional forces which could hold their ground in any conventional war, but when they were not forthcoming it reduced the ground force goals and charged the ground forces, equipped with tactical nuclear weapons, with the function of the shield and the strategic nuclear weapons with that of the sword. There was then no longer any suggestion of fighting a conventional war; that the sword would be wielded at the outbreak of hostilities was implicit in the doctrine of massive retaliation enunciated in January 1954.[1] There was some modification when the concept of the pause was introduced. It means that after the first tactical nuclear salvo has been fired by NATO ground forces and the attacker has been convinced that the West will use nuclear weapons, he might pause and possibly choose to negotiate rather than fight an all-out war, but it is also understood to imply that NATO troops will hold the enemy and enforce a pause long enough to allow the type of attack to be identified and to trigger off Allied strategic nuclear retaliation in case of a concerted attack. In any event there would be a pause before NATO responded with full-scale nuclear force. But the development of thermo-nuclear weapons and the advent of intercontinental ballistic missiles, coupled with nuclear parity of the two sides, led to a further NATO reappraisal. We have noted before that the non-nuclear forces are now regarded by Britain and the United States as the sword and the nuclear capability is considered the shield. The pause in a non-nuclear attack will presumably be enforced, if at all possible, by purely conventional means,[2] and while the views of the NATO members on the scope for conventional warfare still differ, the trend is towards enlarging it.

The function of the ground forces under this emerging concept is twofold: to strengthen the credibility of the nuclear deterrent by regarding it as the *ultima*, not *prima ratio regum*, and to give the leaders a choice between nuclear and conventional warfare in incidents below the level of an all-out conventional

---

[1] The NATO Council decided in December 1954 to use nuclear weapons if the West were attacked. For the development of NATO doctrine, cf. the detailed account by Robert Endicott Osgood, *NATO, The Entangling Alliance* (Chicago, 1962), pp. 28 ff.

[2] In case of an all-out attack the pause would hardly be longer than two days. Cf. Captain B. H. Liddell Hart. 'The Defence of West Germany and the Baltic', *Marine Corps Gazette*, February 1964, p. 20.

THE SETTING FOR CONVENTIONAL WARFARE

attack. The doctrine of massive retaliation is thus being superseded by the doctrine of the flexible response. The conventional capability does not replace, but complements the limited nuclear war capability.[1] However, there must be no doubt in anybody's mind that NATO will use nuclear weapons if compelled by circumstances to do so.

The purpose of the following inquiry is to find out how conventional forces can best meet a conventional attack in a European war that may at any time become nuclear, or that has already become nuclear but still gives scope for conventional combat, for instance because nuclear exchanges have been restricted to the high seas or to land targets outside the battlefield.

---

[1] Especially Henry A. Kissinger, *The Necessity for Choice*, p. 86, who believes that NATO must be willing to use tactical nuclear weapons first, while Lt.-Colonel Alun Gwynne Jones, op. cit., pp. 9 and 10, advocates that the West must be able to reply to battlefield nuclear weapons but should not use them first.

CHAPTER 2

THE NEW PATTERN OF CONVENTIONAL WARFARE

CAPTAIN LIDDELL HART was once asked what course he would propose if he were Chief of the Soviet General Staff. He stated in reply that he would take Great Britain by surprise with the largest possible airborne force or possibly by an undersea invasion launched from submarine troop carriers. If that plan were turned down, he would drop airborne forces beside the Rhine bridges, thus preserving them for the Soviet advance, cutting off the Allied forces stationed east of the Rhine and blocking the move-up of Allied reinforcements. He might also suggest a drop on Denmark and the south coast of Norway in order to capture the outlets from the Baltic for the passage of Soviet submarines, and possibly propose another drop on the Alpine passes leading from Austria into Italy. Once the western part of the Continent had been overrun, an invading army would push across into Britain or, possibly, use atomic and bacteriological weapons against her. By her quick annihilation the Americans would be deprived of a base for counter-attack and, given ample time to cool down, they would eventually conclude that they had more to lose than to gain if they tried to recapture their hold on Europe.[1]

Thus spoke Captain Liddell Hart from the other side of the hill before Germany had rearmed and prior to the advent of intercontinental missiles, the hydrogen bomb and the multiplication of atomic weapons. In 1960 he would have stated that in view of the Western Powers' nuclear capability he had no plans for a large-scale invasion of Western Europe and was only thinking in terms of a sudden pounce of a limited kind.[2] It appears, though, that there is one important element in the discarded plans that should be resuscitated, and that is the extension of the battlefield into the opponent's hinterland.

It seems indeed unlikely at the present time that a massive conventional attack would be launched against the West because

[1] *Deterrent or Defence*, pp. 4 ff.   [2] Ibid., pp. 55 and 92.

such a move would precipitate all-out nuclear response.[1] Still, even a sudden pounce of a limited kind could be the prelude to a major conventional war, but on any reasonable assessment a nibbling war, followed perhaps later by other similar moves, seems more likely than an undertaking on a high level.

A conventional war could break out in Europe for a number of reasons and in various ways. A border incident may grow into something bigger. So might unrest in a satellite State. There may be an attempt at politically corroding a NATO country and instigating civil war which an aggressor would then support militarily. Armed conflict may develop over Berlin. There may be a lightning attack on a NATO member with a limited objective and there may be a more ambitious aggression, perhaps by a satellite, especially if the attacker feels threatened, provoked or tempted. The attack by a satellite might be backed by a Soviet threat of intervention, possibly from the sea, if other NATO forces prepared to come to the assistance. There may be an attack by the East to procure the reunification of Germany. An even more extensive undertaking may be launched in aid of a non-Warsaw pact nation at war. Hostilities might start somewhere outside Europe and the battlefield then extend to Europe. China might push Soviet Russia into war on her side. Finally, a major conventional war could break out if the attacker had perfected anti-missile missiles or established nuclear supremacy by other means. Especially in the former case the attacker might prefer conventional to nuclear war in the hope of capturing a portion of the European industries intact. On the whole it seems likely that a deliberate attack would be launched against the West only if its forces were to a considerable extent tied down elsewhere.

The initial advantage in any conflict lies with the attacker because he can create and exploit surprise. With the advent of nuclear devices the attacker's advantage has become greater still because he has a choice of weapons: he can decide on whether to launch a conventional or a nuclear assault. His opponent must be prepared for either eventuality. Yet if the defence is

---

[1] This risk is so great indeed than an aggressor would hardly surrender the advantage of striking the first nuclear blow, as Hilsman, 'NATO, The Developing Strategic Context', p. 32; Mulley, op. cit., p. 16; and Helmut Schmidt, op. cit., p. 71 point out.

concentrated as it used to be in conventional wars it offers an easy target for a nuclear strike by the enemy, and if it is dispersed as it ought to be in a nuclear war, a concentrated conventional attack might quickly breach the positions of the defence.

The effect of this novel combination of surprise and choice of weapons is heightened if the attacker also exploits the new possibilities of warfare in depth: in a future war heavier weapons and equipment can be carried by air to the rear. Not only must the defence therefore be prepared to repulse a nuclear as well as a conventional attack; it must also be ready to deal with either kind of attack originating from the front, the rear, or from both directions.

The defence in a future war is therefore confronted with problems that were unknown in the wars of the past. The attacker did not then have a choice of weapons. Moreover, warfare in depth was limited. Widespread though it was, it lacked weight, because the forces of the rear were restricted in firepower and mobility. In consequence they could hardly ever launch a rear attack against enemy front troops who are as a rule well armed and well equipped. The effort of the forces of the rear was therefore mainly a subsidiary and not a decisive one. They supported their own front troops but they did not as a rule make the main effort themselves; to provide it was the task of the front troops.

In the last war the forces of the rear supported the army's aims in three ways: in an advance they acted as accelerator, in a retreat they acted as brake, and they isolated and weakened the enemy at all times. This rear war was waged by Special Forces—Commandos and Rangers, SAS and Long Range Desert Group, Chindits and Marauders, Independent Companies and Special Service Force, the Brandenburg Division, Skorzeny's Special Formation and many others—, by airborne troops, sections of the air forces, and by partisans operating in every country overrun by the Axis. Their jobs were manifold, ranging from reconnaissance to harassing and fighting. But their attacks were hardly ever directed against significant enemy concentrations and especially not against the front line.[1] Once they had

---

[1] The question whether rear attacks from greater depth towards your own front will in future become more attractive was first raised by General Hackett, op. cit., p. 11.

reached their target area in the enemy rear, they usually confined their operations to that area and stayed there until they were relieved by their advancing troops or could slip back to their own lines.

If we disregard the reconnaissance and harassing forces of the rear and concentrate on the land combat forces, we find that they normally had to take and hold a key objective in the enemy rear. This was the usual Commando and Ranger mission in their land warfare operations: to gain a favourable position for attack or deprive the enemy of a favourable position for counter-attack, to gain bridges or roads or deny them to the enemy, or to remove obstacles in the way of the advancing troops. Commandos and Rangers did not aim at encircling the enemy or wage an attack in strength against his main forces.

The Marauders were not a true rear force but rather an infantry combat team, especially in their attack on Myitkyina, and their operations were therefore not typical of Special Forces. The Chindits originally operated in the enemy's far rear as a harassing force. After General Wingate's death the Second Chindit Expedition moved from the rear towards the front. The Chindits captured Mogaung but it was not their fault that they failed to make a substantial contribution to the campaign effort in the enemy's forward area: not only were they exhausted by then but they were also too lightly equipped to fight successfully against well-organized forces; they were never meant to do this job at all; they had been designed to operate in the far rear.

Soviet Russia had no Special Forces in the last war, and the Japanese Raiding Units were not a combating but a harassing force. The German 'Brandenburgers' usually operated in small units and carried only light arms; they tried to gain and hold objectives in the enemy rear but they never attacked the enemy front line. Skorzeny's Special Formation went only once into action in the combat zone in a major operation and that was in the Ardennes counter-offensive of December 1944; however, its attack against the Allied front was not launched from the Allied rear but from the German front.

None of the Special Forces of the last war were therefore meant to fight against sizeable enemy formations in the combat zone, and the same applied as a rule to the airborne forces of the belligerents. When they engaged in *coups de main*—Fort Eben

Emael, Bruneval—or assisted in landing operations—Oran, Sicily, Normandy—or carried out inland missions—the Germans at the Isthmus of Corinth, the Russians in the Cherkassy-Kiev area, the British and Americans at Eindhoven-Nijmegen-Arnhem—they stayed at their objectives or moved forward, farther away from the front, and not back towards the front where the enemy was strongest. But there were notable exceptions, especially in Crete where the German attack was carried out solely by airborne forces, at the Rhine crossing when British and American airborne divisions smashed the enemy defences from the rear, and on the Russian front when six or more Soviet airborne brigades reinforced their own ground troops which had passed through the gaps in the German front in the Vyazma-Smolensk-Roslawl area in the winter of 1941/42 and were apparently ordered first to cut the German supply routes and then roll up the German front line from the rear. They did not succeed; by June 1942 the Germans had managed to wipe out the enemy forces in their rear.

Lastly, the partisans of World War II were engaged in larger-scale combat operations against front troops in Soviet Russia, Yugoslavia and France. Such operations were only possible where the terrain favoured the partisans; they would not have otherwise had the chance to hold out.

On the whole operations by forces of the rear against important enemy concentrations, particularly towards their own front, were rather exceptional in the last war. Several factors now seem to make such operations more profitable and at the same time more imperative. These factors are:

1. Aircraft are in a future war capable of carrying armoured and motorized forces, minus their heavy weapons, to the enemy rear. We shall discuss later whether troops should move overland or by air into the enemy rear, whether tanks can remain operative for long in view of the new anti-tank weapons, and when supplies can be expected to be maintained. But when conditions are favourable for mounting and sustaining such a rear attack, its weight can in future be much heavier than in the past.

2. The forces of the rear may find the opposition in the battle zone less concentrated than in the past. As we shall discuss later, the opposing forces will in future be more dispersed than hitherto, and that applies even in a conventional war. Since nuclear weapons may be used at any moment, neither side can

afford to build up very large concentrations which would, in fact, invite nuclear attack.

3. Attack in the combat zone from the rear, in conjunction with a frontal attack, gives the attacker the chance to distribute his striking forces over front and rear, that is he can disperse them over a wider area without diminishing the impetus of the attack. This form of warfare offers the attacker the only possibility of limiting concentrations at any one point of attack. In theory the attacker can halve the striking force at the front by shifting half the weight of attack to the rear and attacking simultaneously from both sides.

4. Rear warfare in the combat zone therefore gains in significance. The attack has as much weight as hitherto, but it is directed against a less highly concentrated enemy, and the attacker can keep his concentrations limited. In World War II tanks, motorized infantry and heavier artillery could attack an enemy in his rear only after these forces had broken through his front or moved round the flank into his rear. The attack originated in either case, as a rule, from the front, and it became two-pronged in the course of the engagement. If the air landing succeeds, the attack can in future start in the rear or start simultaneously at the front and in the rear. Whatever its size, the rear becomes a battlefield right from the beginning. The rear forces have a better chance than hitherto, and a better chance than the forces from the front, to compel the enemy to a sudden change of front; they thus have a better chance to disorganize him.

In consequence they can, in theory at least, more often make the main effort themselves. The advantage resulting therefrom is obvious: the enemy will be reluctant to introduce nuclear weapons and use them against forces in his own rear because he would endanger his supply and retreat routes by doing so. The rear forces can therefore take greater risks and form larger concentrations than their forces at the front can do, especially if they can channel their attack along the enemy supply and retreat routes.

The attractiveness of rear warfare on such a level is therefore evident. To what extent is it considered feasible by the great powers?

As far as the Soviets are concerned, their most recent openly published literature discusses only nuclear, not conventional, warfare. In nuclear war, however, they attribute to rear operations a very much greater importance than they or any other belligerent did in World War II. In an article in the leading Soviet military journal, the *Military Herald*, Colonel I. Baz pointed out that the dependence on rear services will in future be even greater than in the past; victory is in fact 'utterly unthinkable' without a highly organized rear. Both sides in a future war will therefore aim from the very beginning at paralysing the rear of the opponent and protecting their own rear by organizing reliable anti-aircraft, anti-paratroop, anti-atomic, anti-chemical and anti-bacteriological defence. In consequence, he points out, military science and military leaders have the extremely complicated task of deciding the correct allocation of armed forces and equipment to conduct the battle at the front, the operations in the enemy's rear and the defence of their own home front.[1]

Colonel Baz, it should be noted, was thinking of the far rear, not the combat zone. As far as the latter is concerned, Soviet military strategists considered at first the future employment of airborne forces very much on World War II lines, with nuclear targets added to their assignments. Thus General Magelov, writing in the *Red Star*, and Major-General Rudakov, in the *Military Herald*, list as airborne forces' missions the occupation of key points, the removal of obstacles in the way of the advancing troops, the destruction of important objectives, especially nuclear weapon sites, and the occupation of a sector immediately after a nuclear strike. But General Magelov also indicates that airborne forces will in future have to exploit gaps in the enemy lines after a nuclear strike, and General Rudakov stresses that they must, if possible, expand their sectors, that is fight the enemy in the combat zone.[2]

Major-General Pokrovsky has apparently a more extensive employment of airborne troops in mind when he notes that the wide use of helicopters will lead in the near future to significant changes in the character of military transport and the tactics of

---

[1] Translated and reprinted under the title 'Soviet Military Science on the Character of Contemporary War' in Raymond L. Garthoff, *The Soviet Image of Future War* (Washington, 1959), pp. 96 ff., and under the title 'The Characteristics of Modern War' in *Survival* November/December 1959, pp. 180 ff. The article appeared originally in June 1958.

[2] Cf. Bruno Maurach, 'Die sowjetischen Luftlandetruppen', *Revue Militaire Générale*, October 1962, p. 373 ff. The articles were originally published in December 1957 and July 1960.

troops operating in the enemy's rear; however, he does not define these changes.[1]

A more specific combat function is allocated to the airborne forces in a recent book on Soviet strategy, edited by Marshal Sokolovsky, and it is probably true to say that the doctrines expressed there represent the current views of the Soviet planners.[2] This book too discusses the role of airborne forces in the context of a nuclear war. It envisages frequent movements of troops to the enemy rear; tank troops, motorized troops and special airborne troops will be brought there by air.[3] Air transport, it is stressed, has the advantage that it surmounts 'obstacles in the form of vast zones of destruction and radioactive contamination' and offers the most suitable method for accomplishing manoeuvres in modern war. While the special airborne troops will capture, retain or destroy missile, air and naval bases and other important objectives in the rear of combat theatres, tank and motorized troops will go into action in the combat theatre itself and attack surviving formations in the rear.

The size of these rear operations must obviously depend on the strength of the surviving enemy units and especially those which can only be attacked from the rear because of the effects of the nuclear strikes at the front. But while it is not stated whether rear attack is contemplated even when a frontal or flank attack is possible or whether a joint attack will then be launched from the front or flank on the one hand and the rear on the other, it must be assumed that such co-operation will take place where a combined effort is necessary or desirable.

As the reference to 'surviving enemy formations' implies, these rear missions are in the nature of—possibly larger-scale—mopping-up operations after nuclear strikes, and it must therefore not be taken for granted that airborne operations on that scale are also planned to take place in a conventional war where even the heaviest preliminary bombardment may not decisively affect the opponent's fighting strength. But two reasons can be adduced for believing that similar operations are planned for

---

[1] Cf. Garthoff, *Soviet Strategy in the Nuclear Age*, p. 161. The original article appeared in 1955.
[2] Marshal V. D. Sokolovsky, *Military Strategy: Soviet Doctrine and Concepts* (New York and London, 1963). The contents of the book are discussed by the present author under the title 'Soviet Military Strategy' in *RUSIJ*, August 1963, Vol. CVIII, No. 631, pp. 270 ff.
[3] At present only light tanks are air portable.

conventional war as well. Firstly, airborne operations are as a rule not more and often less risky in a conventional war than in a nuclear war. Secondly, the Soviet belief that airborne operations offer the most suitable method for accomplishing manoeuvres applies to nuclear and conventional warfare alike.

The Soviets apparently think of using helicopters and transport planes for moving the airborne troops. Before their arrival the dropping zones and landing areas will be 'attacked with rockets and bombs by cannon firing fighter-bombers. During the operation additional high-performance aircraft provide cover for the attackers while long-range combat planes isolate the area from enemy interference. After the paratroops have landed, all-weather air support is available for the duration of the ground action.'[1]

How does the West view operations of this nature? General Ridgway, writing in 1956, stressed that forces must be capable of moving by air into the zone of mass destruction at such velocity that the enemy will have no time to recover or to bring in land forces from elsewhere. At the same time, he went on, offensive actions by our airborne and armoured units must further confuse, disrupt and paralyse the enemy by hit-and-run hell-raising deep in his rear.[2] Lt.-Colonel Parson concerns himself with deep penetration which he considers profitable if troops are moved in ground-hugging aircraft.[3] General Gavin points out that airborne operations of the World War II and Korea type are no longer feasible because of surface-to-air missiles, and he advocates the use of sky-cavalry instead.[4]

Lt.-Colonel Miksche regards the value of airborne forces in a nuclear war as only marginal. In his opinion paratroops have moved in the order of importance of forces from second place in World War II to last place in a future conflict. He too believes that operations such as the Normandy, Arnhem and Rhine drops can hardly be repeated in a future war; they were possible, he states, because the enemy air force never really intervened

---

[1] Captain William J. Liell, 'Soviet Airborne'. *Journal of the United Service Institution of India*, October/December 1962, p. 319.

[2] *Soldier: The Memoirs of Matthew B. Ridgway*, as told to Harold H. Martin (New York, 1956), p. 299.

[3] Lt.-Colonel Nels A. Parson, *Missiles and the Revolution in Warfare* (Cambridge, 1962), p. 117.

[4] Lt.-General James M. Gavin, *War and Peace in the Space Age* (New York, 1958), p. 271.

THE NEW PATTERN OF CONVENTIONAL WARFARE

but it will certainly do so in a future war; huge air convoys cannot escape detection, and especially heavy transport will be at the enemy's mercy; the enemy air force will also prevent the opponent's troops from assembling, and it will subsequently cut them off from their supplies. The effects of nuclear strikes by either side—the attacker can isolate the dropping area, the defence can fire nuclear anti-aircraft rockets and air-burst nuclear bombs—would apparently cancel each other out and not give the paratroops any advantage. If dropping zones were dispersed over wide areas and the risks of detection and nuclear strikes by the enemy thus reduced, the effort would be dispersed, the attack deprived of decisive punch, and the operation would degenerate into a mere large-scale guerrilla action.[1]

Mr Dinerstein, on the other hand, thinks that 'in addition to the many special tasks performed in World War II, airborne troops of the future may be used to put newly established enemy missile bases out of operation.'[2]

It will be noted that there is little common ground among Western strategists and no clear picture emerges of the expected contribution to the war effort from rear operations in the combat zone. There is, however, one illuminating statement in an article by Brigadier W. F. K. Thompson on the chances of enemy air forces getting through in a conventional attack; estimated attrition rates of anti-aircraft defence against attack in forward areas of eighty per cent 'are spoken of'.[3] The West, it must be concluded, might accept such losses in exceptional circumstances, for the execution of a particularly important mission, but it would not usually conduct airborne rear warfare operations resulting in such disruptive and suicidal losses.

Yet it appears that we must think about the problem again. Unless it can be solved it seems almost impossible to deploy troops effectively in a conventional war without exposing them to the gravest risks if the other side suddenly introduces nuclear weapons. This observation applies not only to the deployment of the attacker but also to the defence.

The problem will be discussed in Chapter 5.

---

[1] Lt.-Colonel F. O. Miksche, *Atomic Weapons and Armies* (London, 1955; New York, 1959), pp. 190 ff.
[2] H. S. Dinerstein, *War and the Soviet Union: Nuclear Weapons and the Revolution in Soviet Military and Political Thinking* (London and New York, 1959), p. 255.
[3] Brigadier W. F. Thompson, 'Forgotten Factor in NATO Strategy', *Daily Telegraph* (London), March 5, 1962.

CHAPTER 3

DEPLOYMENT IN NUCLEAR WAR

MOST Western writers are agreed that in a conventional war between nuclear powers the troops must be deployed as if they were fighting a nuclear war.

The motif of this school of thought is this: since the belligerents in a conventional war can never be sure that the opponent will not introduce nuclear weapons, they must prepare against this eventuality and deploy accordingly. 'It is certain', Lt.-Colonel Miksche states, 'that the shadow of atomic weapons would so govern the strategical and tactical dispositions of either side as to create a wholly new form of war ... whether or not A-weapons are actually used.'[1] Mr Mulley is more specific. 'The prospect is', he says, 'that any fighting will, or should, be conducted, in the first stages at least, by troops deployed for nuclear and not conventional tactics.'[2] Likewise Mr Thornton Read asserts that 'even in a conventional war in the nuclear age, troops would have to be deployed as if nuclear weapons might be used.'[3] Professor Kissinger held the same opinion in 1957,[4] but by 1961 he had become less emphatic and contented himself with saying that tactics would necessarily differ from those of World War II even if no nuclear weapons were used; 'deployment would have to guard against the sudden introduction of nuclear weapons.'[5]

It is, of course, a fundamental rule of nuclear warfare that concentrations must be avoided as far as that is possible, but, says Professor Kissinger, 'the side relying on conventional weapons must remain concentrated in order to have the firepower necessary for defence.'[6] One obvious qualification must be added: firepower is also required for attack. Mr James E. King, Jr., however, believes that fighting in a conventional war

---
[1] *Atomic Weapons and Armies*, p. 218.   [2] Op. cit., p. 148.
[3] Op. cit., p. 100.
[4] *Nuclear Weapons and Foreign Policy*, p. 153.
[5] *The Necessity for Choice*, p. 75.
[6] *The Necessity for Choice*, op. cit., p. 92.

DEPLOYMENT IN NUCLEAR WAR

will be more open anyway and the forces in contact smaller; and since both sides must be prepared for nuclear attack, the concentrations of both sides, apart from their tactical spearheads, will not be significant.[1] Yet one must not overlook the possibility that the attacker is willing to take risks and that he concentrates his forces considerably more than the defence does; in that case the dispersed defence might not have the necessary firepower and could not fight conventionally. Mr Thornton Read comes therefore nearer to the truth when he points out that 'in a battle between dispersed forces, the side which is less dispersed gains an advantage in conventional combat'.[2] This view is not absolutely correct, though; the defence can as a rule afford to be somewhat less concentrated than the attacker, but since in a mobile battle both sides are on the defence here and on the attack there and they constantly interchange their roles, there seems little point in quarrelling with this statement.

A commander who is directed to fight a war with conventional means thus finds himself in a rather unhappy position: he must avoid concentration of his own forces yet they must be less dispersed than the enemy. If both sides observe this last rule, they must constantly outbid each other and concentrate more and more forces, and in doing so they offend against the first rule which demands dispersion. Professor Kissinger is therefore apparently right when he states that 'in a conventional war against a nuclear power the choice is between accepting military ineffectiveness by employing formations which have been dispersed as if nuclear weapons might be used, or courting disaster by concentrating forces'.[3] That both sides suffer under this dilemma is true but it still remains.[4]

There are, in fact, three possible solutions:

1. The use of nuclear weapons is effectively banned for the duration. The war can then be fought on conventional lines.

2. The West gives up the idea of fighting a war conventionally and answers any attack with nuclear weapons.

3. Troops are deployed in such a way that they *can* fight a nuclear as well as a conventional war, and the latter without certain exposure to either ineffectiveness or disaster.

[1] 'Nuclear Plenty and Limited War', *Foreign Affairs*, January 1957, Vol. 35, No. 2, pp. 244–5.
[2] Op. cit., p. 101.   [3] *Nuclear Weapons and Foreign Policy*, p. 178.
[4] That the defender's problem is greater than the attacker's will be seen in Chapter 4.

As for the first alternative, the key word is 'effectively'; the discussion of this question is outside the scope of this book. The adoption of the second alternative would be highly regrettable for the reasons outlined in Chapter 1, and unnecessary if the third alternative is practicable. In the subsequent discussion of this third alternative we try to establish first what is meant by deployment for nuclear war and nuclear tactics. In other words, what are the doctrines of future land warfare operations (below I), what are the tactics (below II), and which rules must therefore be observed for deployment (below III)?

I. The doctrines. It has only very recently been recognized in Soviet writings that there will not be any continuous front line in a nuclear conflict. Leading military scientists in the Soviet Union argued in the 1950's that the zone of combat operations would spread deep into the rear but they still adhered to the concept of a front line. This was the view of Major-General Talensky[1] and Marshal Bagramian,[2] stated in 1955, and of Colonel Baz in 1958.[3] But it was also acknowledged at that time that a future war would be characterized by military operations of manoeuvre,[4] and that contact between the troops in the front line would become loose. Thus Marshal Rotmistrov stressed in 1955 the need of great independence in the operation of troops which must neither look back on adjacent formations nor adhere to the 'presently usual elbowing of neighbour units.'[5]

In 1962, however, the authors of *Military Strategy* declared that continuous fronts had become a thing of the past and that in future there will be no linear defence constructed along continuous zones.[6] Colonel-General Shtemenko, writing in 1963, asserts that it is now a matter of common agreement between military theoreticians that the front line must be regarded as purely symbolic.[7] There is now also general agreement that ground force operations will be carried out in great depth, with decisive aims, at high speed. Battles and engagements will be

---

[1] Cf. Garthoff, *Soviet Strategy in the Nuclear Age*, p. 109.
[2] Garthoff, *The Soviet Image of Future War*, p. 69.
[3] 'The Characteristics of Modern War', *Survival*, November/December 1959, p. 181.
[4] Colonel Baz, ibid.
[5] Garthoff, *Soviet Strategy*, p. 165
[6] Sokolovsky, op. cit., p. 197.
[7] 'Combat Training of Ground Troops for Modern War'. Translated from *Red Star*, January 3, 1963, in *Survival*, July/August 1963, Vol. 5, No. 4, p. 181, and in *Army*, March 1963, pp. 47 ff.

fought at local points[1] or, as the authors of *Military Strategy* express it, only at vitally important regions and centres that will not be demolished by nuclear missile strikes.[2]

While hitherto the troops broke through the enemy front with the intention of seizing the entire zone within the boundaries of the attack, separate units will in future fight independently against other separate units for the possession of key areas and centres. Ground combat operations in land theatres will be conducted by rocket and gun artillery as well as tank and motorized rifle troops; dismounted attack will be rare.[3] The troops, as noted before, will frequently be transported by air, and the importance of special airborne forces will increase considerably.

In the Soviet concept the battle starts with nuclear strikes. Immediately afterwards the other forces go into action attacking on several sectors. Some tank and motorized troops will penetrate by carrying out surprise attacks along the flanks and in the rear, and others will be moved by air to the rear and operate from there.[4] The tank forces can also move swiftly into the areas neutralized by atomic explosions. According to Marshal Rotmistrov, the tasks of these forces will be to smash enemy groups offering resistance and to prevent the rallying of combat forces and the mobilization of reserves.[5]

There is no doubt that this concept requires smaller concentrations in preparation for the attack than were hitherto necessary. Airborne formations can spread their assembly areas and assemble fairly far away from the combat zone. As for the attack itself, its weight is distributed over front and rear. Last, but not least, the forces will go into battle after tactical nuclear weapons have been extensively used and the defence forces greatly weakened.

However, there are definite limits: concentrations cannot be avoided altogether. Before the offensive the attacker will have in his forward area not only a portion of his striking force and part of his reserves but also troops which will stay in the area, ready to meet a counter-attack, infiltration and rear operations by the enemy.

Concentration is also required for the attack, and the Soviets

[1] Ibid.
[2] Sokolovsky, op. cit., p. 197.
[3] Ibid., p. 228.
[4] Ibid., p. 229.
[5] Cf. Anthony Harrigan, 'Tanks in Nuclear War, a Russian View', *Armor*, July/August 1963, p. 41, where an article by Marshal Rotmistrov in *Izvestia* of October 20, 1962, is discussed.

obviously intend to keep their troops concentrated throughout the battle. Colonel Baz, for instance, speaks of swift concentration on the front line and in depth,[1] Marshal Rotmistrov affirms that an 'avalanche' of tanks will be the determining factor in nuclear combat,[2] and the authors of *Military Strategy* envisage large air-drops in great depth.[3] There is one further pointer: Marshal Rotmistrov asserts that, if necessary, tanks can operate independently behind enemy lines without accompanying infantry and, as *Military Strategy* states, they will continue to fight right up to the end of the operation.[4] It may seem doubtful whether they can really operate without infantry flank and rear cover,[5] but it is clear that only compact formations have a chance to survive in the enemy rear and achieve the decisive results expected of them.

It appears that Soviet strategists are less concerned than Western military writers with elaborating maxims for dispersal of their troops, and the Soviet philosophy of war explains this attitude. Their war aims are defined as the defeat of the enemy's armed forces and the annihilation, destruction and devastation of objectives in the enemy rear for the purposes of disorganizing it;[6] both objectives are to be attained simultaneously. The entire Soviet concept is that of a super-Blitzkrieg, initiated and sustained by a strategic and tactical nuclear saturation effort, resulting in a multitude of zones of continuous destruction,[7] and carried forward by extensive mobile offensive operations in land combat theatres, with the aim of defeating the enemy, capturing vital regions and objectives, occupying his territory, and preventing the invasion of the socialist countries.[8] The strategic concept has been described by Mr Alastair Buchan in these words: 'While the initial pulverising duel is taking place between the United States and Russia, it would be the function of the Soviet Army to reach Bordeaux and the Channel Ports (and very probably Kuwait, Cairo, Athens and Rome as well), so that, when the radioactive dust has cleared, Russia can present America with a *fait accompli* which she might have neither the

---

[1] Garthoff, *The Soviet Image of Future War*, p. 57.
[2] Harrigan, op. cit., p. 41.   [3] Op. cit., p. 292.
[4] Ibid., p. 291.
[5] Cf., for instance, Miksche, *Atomic Weapons and Armies*, p. 162.
[6] Sokolovsky, op. cit., p. 195.
[7] Ibid., p. 196.
[8] Ibid., p. 289.

forces nor the will to reverse'.[1] While Soviet strategists realize that their forces will also have to fight defensively in the course of offensive activities, the campaign which they visualize will be characterized by almost continuous Soviet attacks and advances. The troops must therefore constantly remain concentrated. There is no room for dispersal between missions because each mission is at once followed by another one, without interval.

The contrast between the Soviet and the Western posture could hardly be more striking: all calculations of NATO force requirements and NATO force goals are solely based on NATO's need of self-defence. The NATO ground forces, present or envisaged, would be insufficient for waging a sustained offensive campaign.

Western doctrines and tactics therefore differ in certain respects from the Soviet concept. However, as in the East, it is widely accepted in the West that there will be no continuous front in a nuclear war; mobile defence will take the place of the static defence. But this concept has been vigorously attacked by Lt.-Colonel Miksche who finds it difficult to understand those Western tacticians who want to compel the enemy to concentrate but deploy their own troops in loose formations. In his view the enemy striking forces must be confronted with an obstacle which they can surmount only by closing up their formations, and such an obstacle would be a continuous front which he advocates; it should consist of three successive belts.[2] Similarly Colonel Bonin and Major Adelbert Weinstein had proposed earlier in Germany to set up a 30-mile wide static belt, backed by mobile reserves, along the eastern frontier.[3]

The German proposals must be understood as criticisms of the NATO defence strategy of the time (1954 and 1955). The NATO planners had supposedly decided that in case of a Soviet attack the Allied forces would withdraw to the Rhine, cut from there the Soviet lines of communication and carry out strong counter-attacks culminating in a series of encirclements. By contrast the

---

[1] Op. cit., p. 89. Schmidt, op. cit., p. 53 lists as possible Soviet objectives the Channel Coast, Norway, Rome, the Dardanelles and the Middle East.
[2] Cf. *The Failure of Atomic Strategy*, p. 177, and *Atomic Weapons and Armies*, p. 140.
[3] Cf. for the above, Adelbert Weinstein's booklet *Keiner kann den Krieg gewinnen* (Bonn, 1955), throughout; and for a discussion of these proposals Gordon A. Craig, 'Germany and NATO: The Rearmament Debate', in Klaus Knorr (ed.): *NATO and American Security*, pp. 239 ff. and Henry A. Kissinger, *Nuclear Weapons and Foreign Policy*, pp. 288 ff.

German authors advocated a forward defence strategy in order to avoid, or at least make more difficult, an invasion of Germany; NATO has now adopted a forward strategy and with it a more forward deployment of its forces. Lt.-Colonel Miksche is concerned with a different problem. He believes that the Soviet forces are not likely to forgo the build-up of a continuous front along the Iron Curtain while the Western armies would be inadequate to man a continuous front and would therefore hang in the air. As a result the Soviet forces could invade Western territory 'in widely dispersed battle order, with small separate mechanized spearheads, followed by numerous small infantry groups marching rapidly cross country', and while the Soviet forces would remain dispersed, the West would have to operate in more compact order to defend itself against the enemy's infantry.[1] But even if this appreciation of Soviet intentions were correct which in the light of the above discussion here it is not any more, the supply lines of such a force moving ahead 'in two or three 100-mile-wide sectors' would be vulnerable and any well-organized militia could deal in guerrilla fashion with an opponent practising dispersal on such a scale.

What emerges, though, is the differing Soviet and Western conception about what is a suitable nuclear target. For the West, probably fighting on its own soil, worth-while targets will mostly be enemy troops if they are concentrated, while the Soviets, as the reader will remember, also consider as nuclear targets regions and centres, especially if they are 'vitally important'. If the Soviets were confronted with the situation depicted by Lt.-Colonel Miksche, they would stop the infiltration by nuclear area saturation while Western strategists think of keeping their own troops dispersed, forcing the enemy into concentrations and then annihilating him.

Soviet military scientists cannot therefore attribute as much significance, as the Western planners do, to forcing the enemy to concentrate his troops. In fact, such tactics might impede their own advance: it takes time to carry out the necessary manoeuvres; by not attempting them, they save time. It cannot even be said that they save it at the expense of their casualites because they might lose fewer men in a short than in a protracted war.

East and West therefore differ significantly in their doctrines on dispersion and concentration, and that in two respects: Once

---

[1] *The Failure of Atomic Strategy*, pp. 178–9.

the Soviet forces have started the attack, they keep concentrated while the West intends to switch from one form of deployment into the other and back again. And while the West aims at manoeuvring the enemy into concentrations, the Soviets intend to deal with 'surviving enemy formations' as they find them.

However since the Soviet striking forces keep concentrated, they must seek at all times to get so close to the opponent that he cannot use nuclear weapons against them without endangering himself, and where this is not possible they will use tactical nuclear weapons more liberally than the West. This is the essence of their tactics.

In order to enable the troops quickly to concentrate and disperse and also to reduce their demands on supply bases, the West is organizing its forces into smaller, yet still effective, self-contained units. The organization of the various Western forces is not uniform but the aim is everywhere the same.[1] However, smaller dispersed formations find it difficult to hold ground, and especially so in mobile warfare. Professor Kissinger[2] and Captain Liddell Hart introduced the concept of dominating areas instead. In Captain Liddell Hart's words, 'dominating areas is going to count more than capturing or maintaining positions',[3] and General Noiret has amplified this concept by saying that the idea of occupying territory must give way to that of controlling it. 'It can be said to be controlled by friendly forces', he states, 'if the enemy cannot penetrate into it or is destroyed as soon as he penetrates'.[4]

This concept is familiar in guerrilla warfare. Guerrillas do not form a front line; they would be much too vulnerable if they did. Nor do they aim, before they transform themselves into semi-regular and regular forces, at occupying areas; by such tactics they would only squander their forces, consume their strength, and make themselves an easy prey for the enemy. They must remain elusive, concentrate quickly for attack and disperse just as quickly afterwards; mobility is their watchword. They usually operate in small detachments. By their harassing tactics they deny the enemy the possibility of moving freely in partisan

---

[1] Cf. for a survey of the new structures, Mulley, *The Politics of Western Defence*, pp. 140 ff, and Brown, loc. cit.
[2] *Nuclear Weapons and Foreign Policy*, pp. 180–1.
[3] *Deterrent or Defence*, p. 183.
[4] General Jean Noiret, 'Les formes de la guerre et de l'Armée future', *Revue de Défense Nationale*, January 1963, p. 12.

areas, and when their organization becomes stronger they intensify their activities with the result that the enemy is unable to move, first by night and then in daylight as well, in the territory they dominate, and it finally becomes untenable for him.[1] The parallels of these well-tested guerrilla maxims with the doctrine of domination or control are obvious.[2]

Soviet doctrine, however, stresses the importance of capturing and occupying enemy territory, as distinct from dominating it. This is another pointer to the fact that the Soviets are not worried by concentrations of their forces. But it is probably true to say that they take the risk involved because they have to. If they fight in enemy country, their lines of communication are long, and in a nuclear war of quick movement the demand for reinforcements and supplies is heavy. They cannot safely be moved in enemy country unless the forces occupy certain regions and objectives. This is so even if part of the supplies are moved by air.

Soviet strategists, it appears, also differ from the West in their views on how best to deal with enemy nuclear weapons and bases. They seem to favour the *coup de main* for eliminating them. Hence the importance of their airborne forces; one of their tasks, as we have noted, is the independent capture of missile and air bases. The West has, of course, earmarked enemy bases for very special attention too, and the British SAS and the American Special Force are trained to carry out the necessary reconnaissance and attack these targets. But while the Soviets think of 'large air drops in great depth',[3] the two Western forces just mentioned work in small parties. However, the West could also use its airborne forces in this role. It should be noted, though, that the West considers the employment of airborne forces permissible only if they can quickly be relieved, and that would only be the case if the Allied forces were advancing, and even then the depth of airborne operations would be limited. Western planners probably think of destroying enemy nuclear capabilities primarily with nuclear means.

[1] The classic example is supplied by the Viet-minh operations in the Red River delta in 1954. Cf. Otto Heilbrunn, *Partisan Warfare* (London and New York, 1962), p. 64.
[2] Kissinger, *Nuclear Weapons*, p. 180, considers naval strategy as the proper analogy to the above concept of control of territory. One might also refer to air strategy. The fact remains that there is a perfect illustration to be found in land warfare as practiced by guerrillas.
[3] Sokolovsky, op. cit., p. 292.

DEPLOYMENT IN NUCLEAR WAR

The Soviets realize, as Western writers do, that 'in the course of offensive activities troops will be forced into separate offensive and defensive actions',[1] that 'the belligerents in the land theatres will attempt to achieve their aims mainly in offence... Defence will not disappear entirely, but the distinction between offence and defence will not be as clearly expressed as in past wars',[2] that a breach of the defence ' "line" would be met by a series of delaying skirmishes, followed by counter-attack from highly mobile reserves',[3] and that the methods of defence will be essentially the same as those of the offence.[4]

But this is not all. One of General Wingate's maxims was that the answer to penetration is counter-penetration,[5] and this maxim certainly holds good in a contest for the control of territory. This constant interchange between offensive and defensive action will therefore not be confined to the territory held by one belligerent but it will also take place in the rear of the other belligerent. Also the troops must always be able to fight in any direction. It can hardly be maintained in those circumstances that the defence enjoys much of an advantage over the offence. As Mr Roger Hilsman has rightly pointed out, numerical superiority gives an important edge to the side that has it.[6]

There is also a consensus of opinion in East and West about the extension of the future battlefield: it will be characterized by its great depth. This extension is dictated by the great range of tactical nuclear delivery systems, the destructiveness of nuclear weapons and the consequent need for dispersion, the thinning out of the front, and the strategic mobility of the belligerents.[7] An American armoured division, deployed to maintain 4,000 yards' distance between battalion task force perimeters and 6,000 yards between battalion task force centres, spreads out over an area of no less than 600 square miles, equivalent to a 30 miles' frontage and 20 miles' depth.[8]

---

[1] Shtemenko, op. cit., p. 50.

[2] Sokolovsky, op. cit., pp. 289–90.

[3] Roger Hilsman, 'NATO, The Developing Strategic Context', in Klaus Knorr (ed.), *NATO and American Security*, p. 32.

[4] General Noiret, op. cit., p. 12.

[5] Cf. Christopher Sykes, *Orde Wingate* (London and New York 1959), p. 510.

[6] 'NATO, The Developing Strategic Context', p. 32.

[7] General W. Pickert, 'Vom Wert der zahlenmässigen Stärke im Atomzeitalter', *Revue Militaire Générale*, February 1961, pp. 200 ff.

[8] Cf. Lt.-Colonel William L. Boylston, 'Armor on the Atomic Battlefield', *Armor*, May/June 1957, Vol. LXVI, No. 3, p. 29.

Forecasts about the depth of operations differ. The depth of the infantry deployment has been estimated by General Gavin at 100 to 150 miles, with reserves further back.[1] General Noiret speaks of a depth of several hundred kilometres,[2] while General Talensky is of the opinion that it will be at least 300 to 400 miles.[3] The most convincing approach is that of General Gale who states that the depth of the battlefield is now marked by the range of tactical aircraft.[4]

With the immense extension of the battlefield in depth it will be difficult to keep the troops supplied. Much stress is put in Western literature on the required ability of the troops to operate continuously at a high level of efficiency without depending on regularly organized lines of communication, and the solution, already mentioned before, is seen in organizing the forces into the smallest effective self-contained units. But the overall supply requirements will remain the same, regardless of how large or small the individual units are. It has also been postulated that the mobile units must be able to carry all their supplies and maintain their equipment, independently of communication lines, yet, evidently, the more the units move about the higher is their need for resupplies and maintenance.[5] At the same time a lot of fuel destined for delivery may be consumed by the vehicles of the supply services if they have to trace and chase the mobile forces. Whether the Soviets assess the facts more realistically is difficult to say. They stress the importance of penetrating into the enemy's rear, and one of the objectives of such missions has always been the interruption of the enemy supply lines. An even higher value must now be set on operations of this type. As Captain McColl has pointed out, the enemy's 'logistic means of survival' can be more easily determined, located and destroyed than the widely dispersed, mobile forces.[6] The use of aircraft and cross-country vehicles for moving supplies might make the lines less ascertainable but the vulnerability of the bases remains.

[1] Op. cit., p. 137.
[2] Op. cit., p. 13.
[3] See Garthoff, *Soviet Strategy*, p. 109.
[4] General Sir Richard N. Gale, 'A Critical Appraisal of NATO.' (Lecture), *RUSIJ*, May 1961, Vol. CVI, No. 622, p. 159.
[5] The British Chieftain tank can operate 24 hours under battlefield conditions; it carries fuel for moving eight hours at top speed. The German Leopard requires refuelling after ten hours' movement at top speed.
[6] Captain Alexander M. S. McColl, 'Should Logistics Go Tactical in Nuclear War?' *Armor*, January/February 1963, p. 26.

DEPLOYMENT IN NUCLEAR WAR

Both sides will therefore assign an even higher priority than hitherto to the interruption of each other's supply lines and the destruction of bases. Bases can, of course, be destroyed with A-weapons and missiles but these are of little value against supply lines if the enemy does not keep to fixed ground routes. To rely for interference on partisans is not enough; none might be available in the area, and even if their equipment is good enough, they cannot be sufficiently trained in time.

How fire-power will affect movement is difficult to predict. 'If we accept as a basis the tactical development which unfolded during the second half of the last war and introduce atomic weapons into the picture', says Lt.-Colonel Miksche, 'then logical reasoning leads us to the supposition that, under 'normal' circumstances, i.e. in a 'normal' theatre of war and between opponents who are materially more or less evenly matched, a static war is likely to result'.[1] While this may or may not be so, it must be recognized that in nuclear war movement gives the chance to escape destruction which a position is bound to invite. While in World War I safety was in position, it lies in movement in a nuclear war.

Each side will try to reduce the other's fire-power or its effectiveness. It will do so by drawing the fire on mock targets by the use of feints. It will also try to deprive the enemy of targets by keeping in close contact with him so that he cannot use nuclear weapons. The success of airborne operations may sometimes depend on whether the troops can so quickly assemble on the ground and get close to the enemy that he cannot use nuclear weapons. But above all each side will try to destroy the other's nuclear weapons and missile bases.

Each side will also try to bring the other's movements to a halt, especially, as we have stated before, by interference with each other's ground and air supply lines and the destruction of depots. Each side will try to annihilate the other's concentrations.

The success of most of these operations depends to a large measure on intelligence and target acquisition. The reconnaissance means are radar, drones, infra-red, thermograph,[2] interception of messages, interrogation of prisoners, and ground and

---

[1] *Atomic Weapons and Armies*, p. 110.
[2] Cf. on these devices Lt.-Colonel J. T. Quinn, 'Some New Aids to Intelligence', *Australian Army Journal*, July 1963, No. 170, pp. 39 ff.

air patrols. Ground reconnaissance is carried out by Special Forces and regular troops; as General Gale points out, the new smaller units require their own reconnaissance capabilities.[1] 'Reconnaissance elements', Colonel-General Shtemenko states, 'must skilfully locate ruptures and gaps in the enemy's combat dispositions, boldly penetrate his defence in depth, determine the location of nuclear means, fix their co-ordinates and transmit these data rapidly'.[2] It would be surprising if the Soviets would not count on help in this task from indigenous communist partisans; that partisans can be a useful source of information was frequently demonstrated in the last war and especially by Soviet partisans.[3]

In the vastness of the battlefield air reconnaissance will be particularly useful in locating enemy nuclear weapons and bases, observing enemy troop movements and concentrations, spotting supply lines and depots, and especially also in assessing the effect of one's own and the enemy's nuclear strikes; after an enemy nuclear strike the air force may provide the only link between the devastated area and the higher command.

The other functions of the air force are to deliver nuclear weapons, transport troops, weapons, equipment and supplies, give direct battle support, and so on;[4] helicopters will move troops within the battlefield, especially over obstacles. Since ground supply lines are vulnerable and bases located in great depth, some of the supplies will be moved by air. The air force can fulfil its task only if it can establish local air superiority, and the attacker may try to achieve this superiority before the land battle commences.

II. What, then, will be the battle tactics?

The attacker will attempt to get quickly into his opponent's rear. He will make use of feints in order to deceive him about the location of his bases, the area of his troop concentrations and the direction of his main attack, thus trying to draw off enemy forces and fire, he will keep concentrated throughout the battle and seek close contact with his adversary who cannot then use his nuclear weapons.

The defence will carry out delaying skirmishes and counter-

[1] 'The Training of Land Forces', *Revue Militaire Générale*, December 1959, p. 605.
[2] *Army*, p. 52; *Survival*, p. 183.
[3] Cf. Brigadier C. A. Dixon and Otto Heilbrunn, *Communist Guerilla Warfare* (3rd Edition: London, 1961; 4th Edition: New York, 1962), throughout.
[4] For a discussion of air force tasks, cf. Buchan and Windsor, op. cit., pp. 168 ff.

attacks. If a breach cannot be sealed in this way it has been suggested that the defence should try to keep the width of the breach as small as possible, allow the attacker to extend himself in depth, and then cut him off at the break-through point. The attacking forces would then offer lucrative nuclear targets during the break-through and in the narrow neck.[1] But it must not be overlooked that in order to keep narrow the channel of the enemy's penetration and cut him off, defence concentrations are necessary and they offer good nuclear targets themselves. Alternatively, the opposing forces might soon become so intermingled that neither side can use nuclear weapons.

It has therefore been proposed that after the holding forces have pressed the enemy into narrow channels, they should suddenly relax their stranglehold so that they can fire atomic weapons. But such a manoeuvre would still leave them exposed to the enemy's nuclear fire and he might either fire first or, if he prefers, cling to them, enjoy safety from their nuclear fire, and widen his hitherto narrow channel in the process; after all, he cannot be unaware of the purpose of the manoeuvre.

According to another, more elaborate defence concept the attacker will be hemmed in by the pressure of holding forces on either flank, his route of advance will then be barricaded by a blocking force and he will subsequently be struck in the flank by a counter-attack force. The main purpose of the blocking force in this concept is to gain time for the counter-attack force to move up into the area and deal with the intruder. But the blocking force is placed in a particularly vulnerable position since it has to meet the intruder head-on, and should tanks be used on either side in this encounter, the numerically stronger side has the advantage. But apart from the composition of the defence force, should it put up serious resistance the enemy must regard it as a tempting nuclear target even if it is dispersed. The defence, on the other hand, may find it difficult to use nuclear weapons since its holding forces, the blocking force and the counter-attack force are likely to be in the way.

It may therefore seem more attractive to rely less exclusively on mobile defence and introduce some static defence elements instead, viz. confront the enemy with manned obstacles. However, small forts, pillboxes and nuclear hedgehogs, as they have been called, would hardly be suitable. It has been suggested to

[1] Cf. Roger Hilsman, 'NATO, The Developing Strategic Context', p. 28.

site them at such a distance that one medium-yield atomic weapon cannot put more than one of these posts out of action. But while they may be an unattractive target individually, a fortified zone of such defence works would clearly invite nuclear saturation attack and their value would thus be problematic; they would be death-traps. Furthermore, once they are in danger of being overrun they are in the line of fire of their own nuclear guns in the rear. Static defence features have no place on the nuclear battlefield.

Above all, the idea that defensive localities could fulfil a useful purpose ought to be discarded. These localities, it is suggested, should be held by a force not large enough to attract nuclear attention by the enemy, but still powerful enough to compel him either to concentrate in order to storm them or to by-pass them and thereby be led into so-called nuclear killing grounds. In either case, it is held, the enemy would present a nuclear target.

But in the first place, how is the enemy to know that the force is not large enough to merit the expenditure of a nuclear weapon? After all, the force is concealed and he might well believe it to be very much stronger than it really is; in that case he would consider it a worthy target for a nuclear weapon. Secondly, can it really be supposed that the enemy would hesitate to use a nuclear weapon if the alternative is for him to concentrate for an attack on the defensive position, thus presenting a nuclear target himself, and be annihilated in the process? The plain fact is that any position which the enemy can seize only by concentrating is, in his eyes, certainly worthy of his nuclear attention, regardless of how large or small the garrison, and he will seek to destroy it with nuclear weapons.

Apart from that, it should not be assumed that the defensive localities can be so positioned as to make the enemy follow the avenue to a selected killing ground. He will soon enough suspect a trap and act accordingly. In short, the concept of defended localities is not practicable.

The enemy must be stopped by other means. The aim should indeed be to force him into narrow channels and deny him freedom of movement elsewhere. This must be achieved with a minimum of mobile holding forces; primary reliance should be placed on the atomic fire pattern, air intervention, minefields and, where possible, natural obstacles.

DEPLOYMENT IN NUCLEAR WAR

This concept seems to have been adopted by the British Army. 'To offer an effective defence it must rely upon the early use of nuclear weapons and upon artificial obstacles to supplement the hills and rivers. Some of these obstacles are to be provided by a system of Atomic Demolition Munitions—a sort of nuclear minefield designed to force the enemy into restricted lines of advance that can more efficiently be defended with the limited resources of the British Corps'.[1] Contrary to the aforementioned schemes, the British concept preserves full freedom for the defence to use nuclear weapons; no friendly troops are in the target area.

The battle might therefore be fought on the following lines: The fight for air superiority starts before the battle, probably already at the beginning of hostilities. The battle itself begins, as we have noted, with a nuclear saturation attack, immediately followed by a massive tank and motorized infantry attack on the flanks of the area of devastation or, if possible, through the area itself, with the aim of mopping up all surviving formations. While these forces try to make their way to the rear on the ground, at a rapid pace, others are air-lifted to the rear and start their operations from there, in any direction, and special airborne forces are landed and dropped near important objectives, such as missile and air bases; the air-landings might be preceded, as Lt.-Colonel Parson has pointed out, by missile artillery attack, by air-mechanized patrols which would seize air-landing areas, and by air-mechanized cavalry which would silence the air defence and block counter-attacks en route.[2]

The attacker counts for the success of his operations on the effect of his nuclear strikes and therefore takes the risk of keeping his forces concentrated throughout the attack; he minimizes the risk by shifting some of the weight of attack to the rear, and also by keeping as close to the opponent as he possibly can. The defence tries to reduce the effect of the nuclear attack by dispersing its forces, weapons and supplies. It will immediately counter-strike with nuclear weapons in order to seal off the battle area, destroy enemy nuclear weapons and missile bases and break up the ground and air attack. It will rush reserves into the devastated areas. The first ground forces to make con-

---

[1] Lt.-Colonel Alun Gwynne Jones, 'Lack of Infantry the Crucial Weakness', *The Times* (London), October 17, 1963.
[2] Op. cit., p. 117.

tact will probably be tanks supported by their organic artillery. The aim of the defence will be either to disperse the enemy tanks and fight them off, or to keep their movement in narrow channels, bring it to a halt with mobile forces and discharge nuclear weapons into the resulting agglomeration. Similar tactics would be used against armoured or motorized infantry coming in from the front while airborne forces would immediately on landing be overwhelmed by tanks, supported by infantry. At the same time each side will try to cut the other's supply lines, keep them cut and destroy the bases. The defence will also carry out counter-attacks in the enemy rear.

This is, of course, an oversimplified picture of a battle and a very tentative illustration of battle tactics in a nuclear war. Several points stand out. Firstly, the outcome of the battle depends to a large extent on target acquisition; especially the location of nuclear weapons and delivery systems must be ascertained. The targets next in the order of importance are probably the supply lines and depots; if they can be put out of action, the attack loses its impetus and peters out. Secondly, superior mobility is all-important. Tanks ought to be air portable so that they can be transported by air to and within the combat zone and to the enemy rear, cross-country vehicles must be amphibious and artillery self-propelled. Thirdly, local air superiority is of the utmost importance. Fourthly, as Field Marshal Lord Slim has stated, 'the essence of the situation is that troops are likely to be cut off from direct land communications with their bases, and the main problem in such instances is apt to be the question of maintaining the right morale'.[1] Finally, control over one's own forces will be most difficult to maintain —destruction and jamming will severely handicap the communication system—and there can be no guarantee that action on the battlefield will conform to the tactical aims of the command.

III. What are the rules for deployment? As far as the attacker is concerned, he will concentrate his forces immediately before the attack. The assembly areas for the airborne portion of the armoured and motorized troops can be dispersed and they can be located at a considerable distance from the front. If the ground assault forces are resupplied in the forward area, they

---

[1] Quoted in *The British Army in the Nuclear Age*. By an Army League Study Group of which Richard Goold-Adams was Rapporteur (London, 1959), pp. 27–28.

can assemble at various points at a night's march distance from the front; since modern tanks reach maximum speeds of up to 40 m.p.h., their distance could be considerable. In such a deployment the most forward elements would be those that remain behind to meet an enemy counter-attack and secure the area. Their deployment and that of the artillery would be similar to that of the defence.

The defence must be so deployed that it can meet an attack from the front, the flank and the rear, and that means deployment in chessboard fashion. A flank attack might develop quite suddenly: the enemy may have succeeded in infiltrating through the dispersed defence or in moving swiftly through an adjoining devastated area. Similarly, a rear attack might start without much warning after a successful enemy air-landing in the sector.

The rather deep forward areas will probably be thinly manned in order not to attract nuclear fire; furthermore, the forward communication lines are so vulnerable that large forces could not be kept supplied.[1] The main task of these covering forces will be to act as observers and especially to identify attacks. These troops should be equipped with anti-tank weapons and possibly with medium and low-altitude air defence weapons, and there should also be some close-support tanks. The forward area is backed by an imaginary contact line. Behind it is the battle area where the holding and counter-attack forces—the first mostly infantry, the latter armoured formations—will be deployed in much greater depth, in smaller units, and more dispersed than hitherto. These forces must be able to fight the enemy wherever he may appear on the battlefield. Gaps between them will be covered by nuclear weapons.

The nuclear deployment pattern therefore provides for a more even spread of armour across the vast battlefield. Infantry is required to prevent infiltration, accompany tanks, protect the artillery and the missile bases, and to keep its sector under control. It is also needed for the counter-offensive, especially the silent night attack. Most of it will be found in the forward and intermediate zones, and it must necessarily be mobile too; when stationary it will dig in.

Each battle group must be small but still capable of fighting

---

[1] Major-General Hamilton H. Howze, 'The Land Battle in an Atomic War', *Army*, July 1961, Vol. 11, No. 12, p. 32.

on its own. Distance must be kept from other units in the sector. When General Gavin took command of US VII Corps in South Germany, he had his Staff determine concentrations of troops and supplies per five-kilometre square, a radius of two and a half kilometres being the medium lethal distance of a 50-kiloton weapon, and arranged deployment accordingly.[1] Lt.-Colonel Miksche has suggested that the effect of nuclear weapons can be further reduced by deploying in broad lines or narrow deep columns.[2] But once battle has been joined the tidy deployment pattern can no longer be maintained and it will be most difficult in practice to keep concentrations to the minimum postulated in theory.[3]

The mobile reserves should be kept beyond the confines of the possible combat area and at least a portion of them must have air transport available.[4]

The need for reinforcing the mobile forces by semi-static local forces in such an enormous battle area and the far rear is obvious. Marshal of the RAF Sir John Slessor was the first to suggest that locally maintained Home Guards should be formed for this purpose; they should be armed with anti-tank weapons and light automatics and cover the whole of Germany. They should lay minefields, block roads, destroy tanks and armoured carriers, and be in charge of demolitions.[5] Likewise Captain Liddell Hart has advocated that such militia-type formations be created, organized to fight offensively and defensively in guerrilla-like warfare and also able to man a deep network of defence posts in the forward zone and act as a check on an enemy airborne descent.[6] Germany is at present building up a militia force which it is hoped will number 50,000 by 1966. Its tasks are to secure the operational bases of all NATO units stationed in

---

[1] Cf. General Gavin, op. cit., pp. 136–7.

[2] Cf. for particulars *Atomic Weapons and Armies*, p. 131.

[3] It is in the circumstances important that the units in a sector can keep in direct radio contact with each other and, if possible, also with the air force. Otherwise they might kill friend instead of foe with their nuclear fire.

[4] The size and composition of the forces allocated to the various sectors will of course differ from sector to sector and depend on the appreciation of the enemy's intentions. About the likely invasion routes in West Germany, cf. Liddell Hart, *Deterrent or Defence*, p. 171. For the Howze Report on battlefield air-transport, cf. *Army, Navy and Air Force Journal & Register*, Sept. 29, 1962.

[5] In *Strategy for the West* (London and New York, 1954), p. 77, and in 'Britain and the Threshold', *Daily Telegraph* (London), September 7, 1962

[6] In *Deterrent or Defence*, pp. 65 and 172.

West Germany, to give logistical support to such units, and to help with German civil defence.[1] It appears that this militia will not come under direct NATO control in case of an emergency;[2] it is obvious that it should.[3]

How will the artillery be deployed? Even in a nuclear war conventional artillery has not become obsolete; it has to do the job where nuclear devices will not be used because the troops of both sides are in close contact or the target does not warrant nuclear attention. In view of the much larger range required, gun artillery must to some extent be replaced by missile artillery, as East and West recognize[4]. On the other hand, as Colonel Parson points out, in close support gun tubes are superior to missiles in rate, quality and precision of fire support.[5] The light artillery must be able to go with the first-line forces.[6] Medium and heavy artillery must be moved for safety reasons as far back as possible and must give support from greater depth than hitherto;[7] the range of these guns must be increased, and so must be their mobility. Guided anti-tank missiles must be spread all over the battlefield. Light tank destroyers will be used in a mobile role; so presumably will the armoured carrier/launchers and the amphibious armoured cars with anti-tank missiles.

The density of gun and missile artillery dispositions will be less than it used to be because firepower will now chiefly be supplied by nuclear delivery systems and aircraft equipped with air-to-surface missiles. Missile artillery and anti-tank rockets can be dispersed, and the same applies to anti-aircraft guns. Nuclear artillery can be even more widely dispersed because of its enormous destructive capability. Lt.-Colonel Miksche has calculated that in order to achieve an adequate effect along the entire front and to cover all possible sectors against attack, it is sufficient to place individual guns at a distance of four to six

---

[1] Cf. announcement by the Defence Minister, Herr von Hassel, *The Times* (London), of August 6, 1963. For the French forces de défense opérationelles du territoire which have combat and partisan tasks, cf. Pierre Messmer, 'Notre politique militaire', *Revue de Défense Nationale*, May 1963, pp. 751 ff.

[2] Cf. Oberst Schuler, 'Die Landesverteidigung in der Bundesrepublik', *Revue Militaire Générale*, March 1963.

[3] Heilbrunn, 'Soviet Military Strategy', p. 272.

[4] Cf. Sokolovsky, op. cit., p. 227; Gavin, op. cit., pp. 137–8.

[5] Op. cit., p. 126.

[6] Ibid., p. 125; Marshal of the R.A.F. Slessor, *Strategy for the West*, p. 77.

[7] Parson, Op. cit., p. 125.

miles from each other and six to eight miles behind the front; if their range is 25 miles, the fire of four or six guns can always be co-ordinated on threatened sectors.[1]

An artillery belt, stretching 3,000 to 6,000 yards deep behind the front, has no longer a place on the nuclear battlefield.

What the aims of the new warfare should be, is a matter of contention, at least in the literature. The Soviet aims, as already mentioned, are the defeat of the enemy's armed forces and the disorganization of his rear by annihilation, destruction and devastation of rear objectives. The British and American aims are the same for nuclear and conventional war: the destruction of the enemy's will to fight in the British formula, and the destruction of the enemy's armed forces and his will to fight in the American definition. But the question has been raised in the West whether nuclear war does not require its own peculiar set of aims. It has repeatedly been pointed out that a limited nuclear war can only be kept limited if the enemy is not brought to his knees lest he initiate general nuclear war in desperation; there must be neither total victory nor unconditional surrender, or, as the US *Army Field Manual* 100–5 expresses it under the heading 'Limited War': 'Limited war presents a double problem. On the one hand aggression must be opposed, met promptly, and dealt with forcibly. On the other hand force must be applied so as to minimize the risk that the conflict will expand to general war'. But what the aim should be on the battlefield, has remained vague.

It must in fact be what it always was: to win that battle. There is no substitute for victory on the battlefield. Otherwise the enemy will win. Once battle has been joined it must be brought to a successful conclusion. But the advent of nuclear weapons has brought about a significant shift in purpose: 'The object in the land battle in a nuclear age is no longer to capture your enemy; it is to destroy him with atomic weapons',[2] and, again, 'not the mere holding of ground, but the destruction of enemy forces must be the military objective'.[3] It is only in the exploitation of victory that moderation can be shown.

---

[1] *Atomic Weapons and Armies*, p. 133.

[2] Field Marshal Viscount Montgomery, 'The Panorama of Warfare in a Nuclear Age' (Lecture), *RUSIJ*, November 1956, Vol. CI, No. 604, p. 506.

[3] General Sir Richard Gale, 'The Training of Land Forces', p. 607.

DEPLOYMENT IN NUCLEAR WAR

In a—limited—nuclear war the Western defence may limit its strategic aims but it does not seem to have a choice of operational aims; it must destroy the enemy's armed forces on the battlefield.

PART II

A CONCEPT FOR CONVENTIONAL WARFARE

CHAPTER 4

DEPLOYMENT FOR CONVENTIONAL WAR

WE have tried in the preceding chapter to trace the pattern of deployment for a nuclear war. How does this pattern suit the requirements of conventional war?

Three characteristics typify the nuclear battlefield: the defence is mobile, the battlefield is vast, and the troops, under the NATO concept, are dispersed.

The three forms of defence—linear defence, position or area defence, and mobile defence—have all been applied in past wars, though often in a somewhat diluted form. The linear defence of World War I adopted some features of position defence, and the mobile defence of World War II usually incorporated elements of the position defence. Mobile defence in a nuclear war, however, is purely mobile and does not borrow any static defence attributes: it relies solely on manoeuvre, fire and the use of ground for the destruction of the enemy.

Linear defence in form of the continuous trench line came into its own in World War I. Long before then it had been regarded as a most unfortunate form of defence. Napoleon had pronounced against all forms of static warfare and particularly against trench warfare: 'he who remains in his trenches', he wrote in 1793, 'will be beaten',[1] and earlier Frederick the Great had insisted in his *Generalprinzipien* that the line 'is useless because it stretches over more ground than there are troops available to man it. If it is attacked in several places it can be overwhelmed with certainty. It does not therefore secure the area and merely deprives the defending troops of reputation and honour'. Frederick relied on relatively small formations of mercenaries for his warfare, and the continuous line requires mass armies to man it. But when they emerged with the French Revolution, his verdict had not entirely lost its validity. Indeed, when in the American Civil War the Confederates extended

[1] Quoted by Major-General J. F. C. Fuller, *The Conduct of War, 1789–1961* (London and New Brunswick, N.J., 1961), p. 52.

their Petersburg line of trenches to such an extent that they could not garrison them any longer with sufficient forces, General Grant was able to break through their front. However, when sufficient forces were available 'it was the rifle bullet and the spade which made the defensive (in that conflict) the stronger form of war', as General Fuller notes, and he quotes two participants in that war who asserted that a man behind an earthwork was equal to three men outside it.[1] The great defensive power of field entrenchments, combined with wire entanglements, machine guns and quick-firing artillery, was again demonstrated in the Russo-Japanese War.

When World War I began there was no shortage of armed manpower in the Allied camp, mainly engaged on one front only; there were, in fact, nearly ten men available per yard of frontage.[2] In the short period of open fighting in Belgium and France both sides had tried to outflank each other and to break through the opposing front; the lines had therefore to be extended to the sea and gaps in the front to be closed if the ground was to be held firmly as both sides insisted that it must. 'Although many lessons of this campaign are yet untested', the Chief of the German General Staff, General von Falkenhayn, wrote on November 16, 1914, 'one has been established beyond doubt, and that is "Hold what you have, and do not yield an inch of what you have won". This is the lesson which I will observe and, as I said, I do not intend voluntarily to cede one foot of ground in the West'.[3] Almost identical words about the need to hold every inch of ground were uttered by Allied commanders. What is more, two months earlier the British C-in-C, General French, had ordered that the line then held was to be strongly entrenched. The scattered trenches were then joined up and formed a continuous line.

While the Allies regarded the continuous trench line as the best device for stabilizing the front and stopping any further German advance, General von Falkenhayn—possibly with the lessons of the American Civil War in mind—realized that the trench line offered him an important advantage of a different

[1] Ibid., p. 105.
[2] Cf. *History of the Great War, Based on Official Documents. Military Operations, France and Belgium 1914.* Compiled by Brigadier-General James E. Edmonds (London, 1933), p. 431.
[3] Cf. Reichsarchiv, *Der Weltkrieg 1914–1918. Die militärischen Operationen zu Lande.* Fünfter Band (Berlin, 1929), p. 585.

kind: the trenches could be thinly, yet still effectively garrisoned[1] and troops could therefore be made available for Germany's eastern front against Russia. Greatly increased fire-power now favoured the defence to such an extent that entrenched infantry could fight off an attack by a numerically very much stronger enemy who had to advance over open ground. The Germans saw to it that they were always on higher ground than the Allies.

It was not for long, though, that the defence was conducted upon a single line; it soon gave way to a series of lines and then to a series of zones, and barbed wire was much in evidence. Before the German main line of resistance there was the forward zone, about half a mile deep; behind it was the battle zone. The rearward boundary of the battle zone was marked by another line which protected the artillery. Still further to the rear was the assembly area for the reserves, and behind it was the rearward battle area.

The front line troops carried out an immediate counter-attack, before the enemy had time to organize his defence, if the situation could thus be restored. Otherwise a prepared counter-attack was waged by the reserves.[2]

The various zones were intersected by trench lines. As Captain Cyril Falls has pointed out, 'these great trench lines were not the system of defence, which could have existed without them. Still, as sheer physical obstacles they were formidable'.[3] Machine-gun nests were dispersed in selected tactical localities. The defence in length had to some extent yielded to the defence in depth. It was shown once again that 'the defender proved stronger than the attacker; the combination of bullet, spade and barbed wire crushed every offensive . . .'[4]

There were many 'Lines' in World War II: the Maginot Line and the Siegfried Line, the Jitra Line in Malaya and the Mareth Line in Tunisia, the Mius Line and the Winter Line in Russia, the Gothic Line in Italy, but apart from the Maginot Line they were more typical of area than of linear defence. The Blitzkrieg period of World War II had, however, shown the ineffectiveness of the purely static defence in the face of a mobile

[1] Cf. P. A. Thompson, *Lions Led by Donkeys* (London, 1927), pp. 119-20.
[2] Cf. for the above Captain G. C. Wynne, *If Germany Attacks: The Battle in Depth in the West* (London, 1940), throughout.
[3] Captain Cyril Falls, *The Nature of Modern Warfare* (London, 1941), p. 46.
[4] Major-General J. F. C. Fuller, op. cit., p. 160.

attack since the attacker can always quickly concentrate superior forces at the point of attack. The defence too must therefore rely on strong mobile forces. But the importance of the static elements in the defensive battles of the last war must not be underrated.

Field Marshal Rommel who had played a notable part in the Blitzkrieg was among the first to feel the telling effect of properly constructed and defended positions. 'The British', he said about their defence system at Alam Halfa in August 1942, 'had defended their strong position with extraordinary stubbornness and had thereby delayed our advance ... Such a respite was of immense value to the enemy, for he only needed to hold his line long enough to allow his mobile forces to take up a position from which immediate counter-action could be taken against any German-Italian forces which broke through.'[1]

The Germans themselves who soon afterwards began their long retreat from the outposts of their conquests, adhered almost to the last to the concept of the continuous front. Often it was weakly manned. Sometimes, even, it existed only in the imagination of the planners. General Fretter-Pico was ordered in December 1942 to close a 125 miles' gap between the Don and Donetz rivers with what was called an army sub-group but amounted in fact to less than a weak corps, and he relates with understandable irony that 'it was a cause for reassurance to the Supreme Command to see (on the map) in the gap the flag of the army sub-group regardless of whether or not it had any troops at its disposal'.[2] As late as July 1944 Field Marshal Model, commanding Army Group Northern Ukraine, insisted that 'forward lines must be held at all costs, artillery and armour must be disposed in rear along a defensive line showing no gaps'.[3] But the concept of rigid defence had to give way to that of elastic defence on this front as it had already done on other sectors in the East. Yet in the West the linear concept was never abandoned. The German Army tried to hold Normandy by linear defence, and west of the Rhine as well as on the Rhine itself it

---

[1] Captain B. H. Liddell Hart (ed.), *The Rommel Papers* (London and New York, 1953), p. 276.

[2] General Maximilian Fretter-Pico, *Missbrauchte Infanterie* (Frankfurt am Main, 1957), p. 101. The designation army sub-group (Armeeabteilung) stands for reinforced corps.

[3] Cf. Major-General F. W. von Mellenthin, *Panzer Battles, 1939-1945* (London, 1955; New York, 1956), p. 277.

again relied on linear defence although manpower was completely insufficient. The record shows that, whenever it was possible, Allies and Axis alike usually formed lines of defence or adopted static defence in depth, with mobile reserves in rear, although the flanks were often open in North Africa and the continuity was interrupted by natural obstacles, especially in Italy. This identifiable front formed a secure wall in advance and retreat in World War II, and the same applies to the war in Korea.

What are the advantages of the static defence coupled with mobile warfare? Field Marshal Rommel has pointed out one of them: it allows the defence to delay the enemy's advance and gain time for counter-action, that is for surveillance, decision, and counter-attack. During the German retreat in Russia it happened again and again that Soviet tank forces and infantry which had broken through the German main defence line were counter-attacked, separated from each other, and while the front troops fought the infantry elements, tanks dealt with tanks and the Germans frequently managed to wipe out the intruders inside the defence system. The Germans were helped by the fact that the Soviet infantry did not then have armoured personnel carriers and the German tank forces were therefore often successful in separating it from its tank forces. It is correct, as General von Senger und Etterlin points out, that the German front troops often played only a minor part in these engagements[1] but it must not be overlooked that this was usually due to their numerical weakness. Where they were strong enough, they did act as breakwaters of the attack.

Closely connected herewith is another function of the static defence system: under its protection tanks can be stationed in rear at central points which allow them quick access to any likely path of advance of the enemy after a breakthrough. It is, of course, true that tank forces could be stationed in rear equally favourably if there were no firmly held front but in that case they would often be compelled to engage the enemy in a frontal counter-attack, possibly without advance warning and, other things being equal, the chances of success of either side would be about equal. But if there is a front line, the positional forces on the flanks of the breakthrough can hold on, the wings

---

[1] General M. F. von Senger und Etterlin, *Der Gegenschlag, Kampfbeispiele und Führungsgrundsätze der beweglichen Abwehr* (Neckargemünd, 1959), p. 12.

of the pierced sectors can act like 'cornerstones', as the Germans called them, and the mobile reserves in the rear can therefore attack the intruder at right angles. The resulting advantage for the defenders is obvious as was shown in the German campaign in Russia: their tanks offered the enemy only their front as target while the Soviet tanks had their flanks exposed. If the German flanking attack sometimes failed it was due to the fact that it was launched too near to the front and came under fire of the Soviet artillery; it would have been more often successful, had it started further back.[1]

But the task of the front line is not only to channel the enemy breakthrough forces or slow down his advance but also to stop and repel him where possible. Because there is a defined firm front, the enemy must concentrate his striking forces in a relatively small sector for a breakthrough attempt and make extensive preparations which should not go unnoticed. The forces in the line, by their presence opposite the enemy all along the front, enable their artillery and air force to find worth-while targets and disturb these preparations. Where there is no fixed front, the enemy may be able to penetrate in dispersed battle order, and since the necessary preparations are less noticeable, he can more easily complete them without interference by his opponent and take him by surprise.

It therefore follows that the front line, by its mere existence, also affords better possibilities for observation. An attack can more easily be identified, in particular the strength and composition of the attacking force, the direction of the attack and the enemy's intentions. Even if the attacker penetrates the front, the mobile reserves of the defence and its artillery and air force have therefore a very much better chance to deal successfully with the enemy than these forces would have if the front is merely 'symbolic'.

For the same reasons, viz. early warning and minimization of surprise, the gun line, tanks, reserves, bases, rear installations and supply lines are afforded a higher degree of protection by the front. In particular it is possible to position anti-tank weapons in the forward line at every likely point of contact with the enemy.

---

[1] Cf. von Mellenthin, op. cit., p. 293. However, the enemy must not be given time to consolidate his position, as von Senger und Etterlin, op. cit., p. 63, points out.

DEPLOYMENT FOR CONVENTIONAL WAR

Thus, while the attacker must concentrate prior to the attack, the defence, based on a strongly held front, gains time to concentrate its reserves after the start of the attack and is in a good position to make full use of the firepower of the defence system and the mobility of its garrison.

The front plays its part not only in the defence but also in the attack. It provides the cover under which the assault forces can assemble, and it gives a firm protection when the attack gets under way. It prevents enemy infiltration and penetration into the rear of the attacking forces and assures continued support for the attack. In particular, by bringing up the forward line and setting up there a continuous belt of anti-tank weapons, the attacker can secure the ground gained step by step against armoured infantry and tank counter-attacks. This tactic was most successfully applied in the last war by the Red Army in the later stages of its advance; its anti-tank guns were placed at only twelve yards' distance from each other. The front provides of course the same advantage for troops equipped with anti-tank rifles. The Germans considered this step by step advance of the continuous anti-tank front the most dangerous element in the Soviet attack.[1]

However, the front line is more valuable for the defence than for the offence. Since, as we have seen, an impending attack can more easily be identified, it has to overcome three successive hazards: to be paralysed at a great distance from the opposing front, to be repelled by the opposing positional troops, and to be counter-attacked by the mobile reserves, possibly in conjunction with front troops.

The front affords the defence with two further significant advantages over the attacker: Firstly, the defence can stay on the defensive in face of an attack until the reserves mount a counter-attack after a breakthrough. But even then the rest of the defence forces can stay on the defensive, for a while at least if the counter-attack fails and indefinitely if it succeeds (below, I). Secondly, the attacker needs great superiority to break through the defensive belts (below, II).

I. What, then, is the advantage of staying on the defensive?

The defence is often entrenched and protected, the positions are camouflaged and possibly fortified, they are linked by mine-

---

[1] Cf. von Senger und Etterlin, op. cit., p. 54.

fields covered by fire and other obstacles, the features of the terrain are made use of and may provide the defence with excellent facilities for observation. The defence system is arranged in depth, the troops and weapons are so distributed that the main strength can quickly be concentrated on the likely path of the enemy's advance, and reserve and support forces are so stationed in rear that they are out of enemy artillery range but can speedily reach any danger point. The artillery and heavy infantry weapons are deployed in such a way that their fire can do maximum damage wherever wanted, and alternative emplacements can be prepared, either in the gun line if their position is fired upon or further rearward if an enemy breakthrough makes it advisable. The batteries can place a barrage in no-man's-land at the start of an attack in order to block the advance of successive waves, they can hit any point there and bring to a halt or disorganize the attack before it has reached the forward zone. Fire into the gaps between strongholds, boxes and resistance nests can often be observed. Forward observation posts can be carefully sited and camouflaged. In short, the entire defence system is so arranged that the best use can be made of the strength of its components. Communications and the supply system can be properly established and tested, especially since command and observation posts, units, artillery emplacements and depots are all more or less static. Everything, as it is, is pre-arranged and stabilized, if only for a limited period.

The attacker enjoys few of those advantages. He may have to move in the open, thus fully exposing himself to the fire of the defence, he may run up against unexpected obstacles and have difficulties in surmounting known and unknown ones, he is swept by fire from concealed and fortified positions, the cohesion of the assault force may suffer and tanks and infantry become separated. His reinforcements may be cut off by an artillery barrage. His own covering artillery fire will be reduced in effectiveness if it cannot be observed, if the assault forces progress unevenly, or if they outrun the range of their guns which must first be brought forward, to unprepared emplacements, before they can fire again. The same applies to anti-tank and heavy infantry weapons, and the dispositions of the defence might deny them the use of favourable ground. Immediate counter-attacks often cannot be harassed by observed fire. The attacker can easily fight himself to a standstill in those circumstances and use up his resources, while the defenders conserve their strength.[1]

II. Because of the above factors the attacker needs more forces than the defence to succeed. Captain Liddell Hart, who pioneered the research into this question, found that the number of troops required to hold a front of any given length has steadily declined over the past 150 years; the defence has been gaining a growing material ascendancy over the offence.[2] Captain Liddell Hart has also come to the conclusion that mechanized warfare has brought no radical change in this trend.

In 1915 a German division in the West held a front of 4 to 6 miles, that is there were 3,000 to 4,500 men per mile of front. Altogether there were 90 German against 140 Allied divisions, yet in spite of an initial tactical superiority of five to one the Allies did not succeed in the great autumn offensive in breaking through. In 1916 and 1917 there were 120 and 140 German divisions against 160 and 180 Allied divisions respectively; still the German front could not be breached. In their spring offensive of 1918 the Germans had 190 divisions against 170 Allied divisions but were unable to break through, and in the autumn of 1918 the Allies, in spite of a threefold superiority, succeeded in pushing the Germans out of successive defence lines but not in breaking them.[3]

As for World War II, Captain Liddell Hart takes his examples from the North African, the Normandy and the German/Soviet campaigns.

As far as the North African campaign is concerned, Captain Liddell Hart excludes from his review those battles where an open desert flank made outflanking manoeuvre possible since, as he stresses, they do not afford a very clear test of defence against attack. Three valid examples are, however, provided by Rommel's attack on Tobruk in April and May 1941, his attack at Alam Halfa in August 1942, and his defence at El Alamein in October of that year. In the Tobruk engagement less than two Allied divisions held a poorly fortified perimeter of 30 miles, that is with 800 men to the mile, against five Axis divisions. At

---
[1] This sentence is taken from the German textbook *Die Führung in der Abwehrschlacht* (1916), as quoted by Captain G. C. Wynne, op. cit., p. 150.
[2] *Deterrent or Defence*, pp. 97 ff.   [3] Ibid., pp. 99–101.

Alam Halfa the opposing forces were of equal strength and although the Allied left flank was open, light forces were positioned there to harass the enemy, should he attack there as indeed he did. He was forced to break off the engagement. At El Alamein the Allies had a threefold superiority in men and a sixfold superiority in tanks; the Axis had 2,000 men to a mile of front. The Allied attack in this decisive battle succeeded but the attacker lost three times as many tanks as the defence.[1]

In the Normandy campaign, Captain Liddell Hart points out, Allied attacks hardly ever succeeded unless there was a fivefold superiority, and when 'the break-out was eventually achieved ... the German reserves were so scanty, and the space for outflanking manoeuvres so wide, that the Allied armies were able to advance almost unhindered.'[2]

Finally, on their eastern front the Germans often held attacks by forces seven times as strong as they, and sometimes even stronger than that; German armoured divisions defended frontages of up to 20 miles.

It is striking, though, that in all these examples from the two World Wars the attack was opposed by a static defence. In World War I it was a continuous trench line or zones intersected by continuous trench lines, and in World War II there were defence zones or belts of defended localities whenever the defence had enough men to garrison them, and the mobile defence forces were stationed in rear.[3] But in a conventional war in which nuclear deployment is adopted, the defence is based solely on manoeuvre; there will be no static elements to act as breakwater. An assessment of the advantages of the defence over the attacker in mobile warfare under nuclear deployment rules cannot therefore be based on previous experience.

It is thus opportune to ask whether the defence would under those conditions still enjoy an advantage over the attacker, to

---

[1] Ibid., pp. 105–6.
[2] Ibid., p. 107.
[3] Cf., for instance, Field Marshal Montgomery's description of the German defence arrangements at El Alamein, in his *El Alamein to the River Sangro*, British Army of the Rhine Printing and Stationery Service, 1946, p. 13. There were three belts of defended localities and minefields in the northern sector, and the less organized defences in the southern sector were sited to canalize any British penetration. Cf. also Field Marshal Rommel's description, quoted above, of the British defence positions at Alam Halfa.

DEPLOYMENT FOR CONVENTIONAL WAR

the same or a lesser degree than in the past, or whether the advantage would disappear altogether.

The purely mobile defence keeps moving much of the time, from the start to the end of the battle; positional troops may stay in their protected positions throughout, and the mobile elements in their rear move out only if and when a counter-attack is required. The counter-attack force in static defence is smaller than the striking force in mobile defence. Furthermore, while the static defence aims at deflecting and stopping the attack within the limited area of the defence system itself, mobile defence is conducted over a very extensive area.

The purely mobile defence is therefore apparently almost as exposed as the attacker; after all, mobile defence must be conducted offensively. However, before the two forces meet, the attacker must move through the forward zone. The defence therefore receives advance warning and the attacker can be subjected to artillery and air force action. Yet the resulting damage to the attacker will often not be great enough to disorganize his forces because he will probably move in tanks and APCs, viz. in protective vehicles, and possibly under cover of low-flying aircraft, and conventional artillery of the defence will neither be concentrated nor plentiful in or near the area.

Once the attacker has passed through the forward zone and crossed the contact line, the defence has a number of further advantages. In the first place, it has a better knowledge of the terrain, it can to some extent choose the point of impact, and it can make use of natural obstacles. It can also surprise the attacker if he is unaware of the defence dispositions. But the attacker has certain advantages too: his troops can appear simultaneously on so many points of the contact line that the defence is thrown into disarray, and if they air-land successfully in the rear as well, the defence may find itself in the same position as if it had an open flank. As the reader will recall, such cases cannot in Captain Liddell Hart's opinion be considered as affording a very clear test of defence against attack.

In mobile defence neighbouring units may often not be able to give mutual support in the same way in which neighbouring strong-points do in position defence. The strong-points are so sited that this support is possible, but in mobile defence neighbouring units may lose contact and can then neither give nor receive support. This may happen especially if they have to deal with several simultaneous attacks by the enemy and are drawn apart in the process.

The defence might, however, benefit from two other factors: its air force operates over friendly territory—which is an advantage—and its artillery is stationed in the area where fighting takes place while that of the attacker must first be brought up. But since the defence artillery is no longer deployed in an unbroken line, the guns cannot just await the enemy's approach in their positions; they must be moved when their brigade moves, and then be grouped together in order to provide effective support. If the time, weight and direction of the attack is unexpected, it may prove difficult for the defence to organize such groups at the right time and place.

It is here where the second characteristic of nuclear deployment, viz. dispersion, makes itself felt. The frontage of a NATO division in Central Europe is at present 30 miles,[1] and if the NATO goal of 30 divisions is reached, the divisional frontage might be reduced to 25 miles. But conventional firepower is geared to a frontage of not more than 10 miles, and if it is drawn out beyond this limit, the effectiveness of artillery decreases sharply.

If a division of three brigades is responsible for a 25 miles' frontage, each brigade has to cover about 8 miles. The brigade artillery will be deployed about 3 to 4 miles back and in a central position in order to cover both flanks with all guns. Their range is something like 7 miles. As a result there will be considerable areas, in the centre of each brigade sector, which will be covered by the organic artillery of one brigade only.[2] (Fig. 1)

Mutual support facility is even further reduced if the division is not deployed in a line but with two brigades up. (Fig. 2)

There is, of course, still the divisional and the corps artillery. The former will be hard pressed if the enemy attacks all three brigades simultaneously, each in its centre, and it will have to change its location if the brigades keep manoeuvring. It will be unable to give support during the period of change, and it may have to move about almost as much as the attacker's artillery. At any rate, it would have to have many more medium guns than in the past because it must supply the fire that has

---

[1] Cf. Buchan and Windsor, op. cit., p. 165.
[2] Cf. for the above and the first chart Otl K. von Beuningen, 'Artillerie Regiment oder Brigade Artillerie', *Revue Militaire Générale*, July 1960, p. 154.

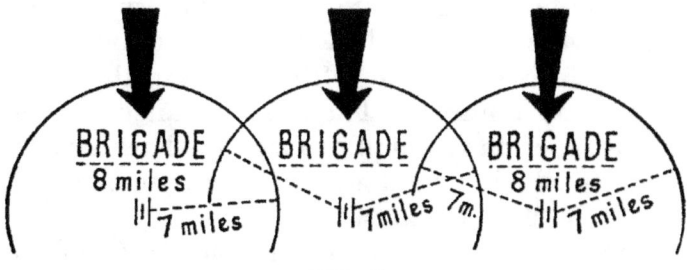

FIG. I

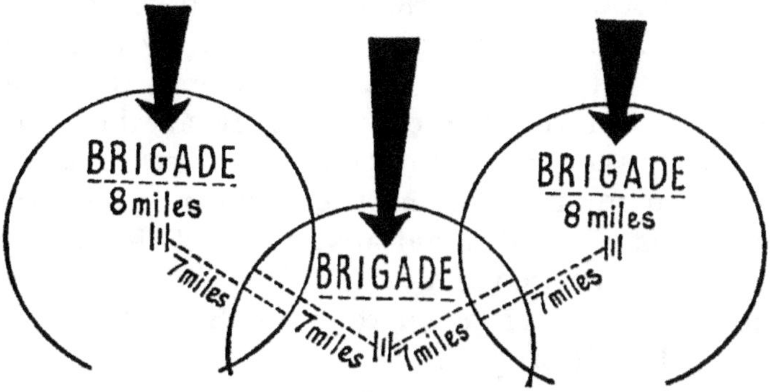

FIG. 2

hitherto been available from adjoining units on the very much shorter divisional frontage. The resulting divisional artillery concentration would probably be so great as to be unacceptable. Furthermore, the range of divisional and corps gun artillery is insufficient to hit the traditional targets, viz. the enemy reserves and the jumping-off areas; they will all be now too far in the enemy's rear. What is needed is a self-propelled gun with a range of between ten and thirty miles.[1]

General Sir Richard Gale states that lacking artillery support can be replaced by adequate tactical air support,[2] and General Howze expects that 'some sort of bombing and strafing aircraft, as an invaluable supplement to artillery, will support land forces' but he states himself that 'the ability of close support aircraft to survive is unknown'.[3] Moreover, a curious situation has arisen in regard to light bombers of the tactical air force which

[1] The Soviets have a 203-mm. gun-howitzer and a 301-mm. gun.
[2] Op. cit., *Revue Militaire Générale*, December 1959, p. 606.
[3] Major-General Hamilton H. Howze, 'The Land Battle in an Atomic War', p. 32.

could attack the targets now out of gun artillery range. Even if these aircraft 'were armed only with high explosive weapons', remarks Colonel Gwynne Jones, 'they exist in the mind of the enemy as nuclear bombers. Their appearance on the radar screens in east Germany might cause the Russians to fear a nuclear attack, which would in turn lead them to fire their medium-range nuclear missiles.'[1]

In the circumstances the defence may not have sufficient firepower and not be able to delay the attacker long enough for its reserves to be brought up while the front still holds. Here the third characteristic of the nuclear battlefield comes in, viz. its wide expanse. The reserves can no longer be stationed at a relatively short distance from the contact line; they may have to move over considerable distances. If at the same time artillery and air support for the defence troops already in contact with the enemy is weak and their power of resistance thus diminished, another traditional advantage of the defence over the attacker has withered away.

Nor should it be overlooked that much of the artillery on both sides will be self-propelled. The attacker can manage more easily than hitherto to bring up his own gun artillery because the forward zone is thinly manned, and since he decides the time and direction of his attack, he may even succeed in having superior fire-power available throughout.

What effect would missile artillery and other missile delivery systems have on the ratio of forces required for attack?

Admiral Buzzard believes that the advent of guided weapons tends to increase the hitherto prevailing defence advantage.[2] He refers in the first place to anti-tank guided weapons which are becoming more and more lethal against tanks, the attacker's main weapon. This is certainly true but the advantage is not entirely one-sided. The defence also relies on tanks, though possibly to a lesser extent, and the attacker will take his toll of the opposing tanks if he succeeds, as the Red Army often did in the last war, in bringing up his anti-tank weapons, or if anti-tank missiles are mounted on amphibious armoured cars—as in the Red Army—or on armoured carrier/launchers—as in the

---

[1] 'Lack of Infantry the Crucial Weakness', *The Times* (London), October 17, 1963. Cf. also Neville Brown, op. cit., *Strategic Mobility* (London and New York, 1963), p. 178, and Thomas C. Schelling, *The Strategy of Conflict* (New York, 1963), p. 247.

[2] Op. cit., p. 19.

British Army—or if tanks are equipped with guided missiles—as the US Army may do—or tank destroyers with rockets—as in the German Army. Furthermore, darkness, fog and smoke protect tanks against anti-tank missiles since they require target observation. Finally, a number of anti-tank missiles are slow in response and flight and some of the guided ones are subject to electronic interference. West and East alike therefore take officially the view that the tank has not become obsolete, in spite of the great advance in those and other anti-tank weapons: in the summer of 1963 the new British main battle tank completed its acceptance trials, the United States, France and Germany brought out new prototypes at about the same time, and we have noted before the important role assigned to Soviet tank forces in a nuclear conflict.[1] If, however, contrary to the appreciations of the planners, tanks should lose their value on the battlefield and the infantry must carry out the attack unaided, the defence would be favoured.[2]

Admiral Buzzard also believes that anti-aircraft guided weapons will usually make an attacker's air interdiction with conventional explosives unprofitable, but this disadvantage is largely cancelled out by the fact that the defence air force will not be able to operate freely over his territory either.

As for missile artillery the defence, fighting in its own area, should do better than the attacker in the way of target acquisition. However, missile artillery cannot yet replace gun artillery in close support, and it is just this ability of the gun artillery which so often in the past made it possible for the defence to defeat attacks by numerically much stronger forces.

It has also been suggested that the great advance in surveillance systems favours the defence because it can make out the pattern of attack at an early stage and prepare in time to meet it. But, as Mr Neville Brown has pointed out, the development of jamming and deception techniques may well deprive the defence of this advantage.[3]

It must also appear highly doubtful whether the defence gains on balance from the more general employment of the

---

[1] Cf., however, Sokolovsky, op. cit., p. 228: 'Today's tanks have become most vulnerable to anti tank weapons, the modern development of which outstrips the development of tanks'.

[2] For a further discussion of the topic, cf. Chapter 6.

[3] Brown op. cit., p. 200.

proximity fuses that make high explosive shells and bombs more effective against troops in the open. The defence, as we stated before, is almost as exposed as the attacker, and probably just as much as he if divisions are assigned very long frontages. The present frontage held by a NATO division is 30 miles. 'A highly mobile division would probably be able to screen twenty-five miles, but the odds it would be able to accept would be less. This is because its success would depend on the frequent launching of counter-attacks at points of penetration and this would entail sacrificing the advantage of resting on the tactical defensive.'[1] That the defence will in future be almost as exposed as an attacker who moves in protective vehicles is the very point so often overlooked when it is asserted that technological developments since the last war have resulted in another shift in favour of the defence.

Thus, while the defence still seems favoured, its advantage has in fact become smaller and at the same time less predictable. It depends on rather uncertain factors, such as the availability of gun artillery for close support in the required strength and at the required time and place, the attacker's skill in waging simultaneous attacks over large areas, and his ability to use tanks effectively and to establish local air superiority.

But the built-in safety devices of the static defence systems which automatically required the attacker to launch his attack with numerically much superior forces no longer operate. All the inherent advantages of the static defence over the attacker are either reduced or gone altogether if *mobile* defence on a *nuclear scale* is adopted: the physical obstacle presented by trenches, defended localities and strong-points arranged in successive belts, the barrier against infiltration which the continuous line provided, the siting of the defences in such a way that mutual support was assured, penetrations were canalized and the attacker could be intercepted within the defence zone, the limited need of the defence to move in the open, the facilities for right-angle counter-attack on the attacker's forces that had broken through, the domination of no-man's land by the defence artillery, its threat to the enemy's assembly areas, the availability of its strong coverage all along the front, its preponderance on the battlefield and its capability to provide concentrated fire.

[1] Brown, op. cit., p. 203.

DEPLOYMENT FOR CONVENTIONAL WAR

What is left of the traditional defence advantages is little enough: the defence receives advance warning of the attack when the attacker moves through the forward zone and can inconvenience him with artillery fire; it has a better knowledge of the terrain, it can erect obstacles, and it can to some extent choose the point of contact; its air force operates over friendly territory and its artillery is, possibly, nearer at hand; its anti-tank weapons may do more damage than the attacker's, and its missile artillery is in a better position to acquire targets. Finally, its supply lines are shorter.

There remain four elements which might favour either side: leadership, initiative, surprise and morale. However, it does not appear that one side or the other enjoys a definite advantage of such magnitude that it would influence the ratio of forces required in a predictable way.

It therefore seems that if the conventional defence adopts nuclear deployment, it must be almost as strong numerically as the attacker.

This conclusion is reinforced by a survey of two Desert Campaign battles where an open flank made outflanking manoeuvres—and hence the extension of the battlefield—possible. In the operation for the relief of Tobruk, the 'Crusader' battle of November and December 1941, the battlefield had a depth of about 100 miles. The Germans and Italians under Field Marshal Rommel had three armoured and seven infantry divisions; the British were of about equal strength.[1] The British took the offensive. Both sides were on the move throughout, and the battle was decided by manoeuvre. The British won it.

In the battle of Gazala, in May and June 1942, numbers in armour and infantry favoured the British. This time Rommel took the offensive. After a thrust round the flank into the British rear to a depth of 30 miles or so, he sat back on the defensive in order to open up a safer supply route; 'while doing so, (he) invited the piecemeal armoured attacks which the British obligingly delivered, whereby he reduced his enemy's armoured superiority to the point where he felt strong enough to resume the offensive',[2] and went on to win. The British defence was based on the Gazala position, a chain of brigade 'boxes' and

---

[1] Cf. Lt.-General Sir Francis Tuker, *Approach to Battle* (London, 1963), p. 21.
[2] Ibid., p. 129.

minebelts, but once again the battle was decided by the forces of manoeuvre.

Both battles are characterized by mobile operations in vast areas and near parity in numbers of the forces engaged. The experience there seems to confirm that while the defence is not safeguarded against defeat by numerical parity, it cannot afford to fight with less in mobile warfare in great areas.

This is so unless there is a revolutionary development in conventional fire-power, designed to increase the defensive capabilities of widely dispersed troops. Brigadier W. F. K. Thompson has convincingly argued the need for weapons of this type. 'In Central Europe', he remarks, 'the nuclear missile is now the dominant battlefield weapon and there is no retreat from that position. The situation must, therefore, be lived with until either general disarmament is accomplished or the position transcended through fresh scientific discoveries. What is most urgently needed is a new breakthrough in weapon development which will produce a controllable mass-effect weapon but without their objectionable features. Such a weapon should enable defence plans based on nuclear tactics to be prosecuted without recourse to nuclear missiles.'[1] Brigadier Thompson also stresses the need for other less indiscriminate weapons which would strengthen the defensive power of dispersed forces, especially anti-tank weapons which would put an end to the offensive role of armour.

We must be clear, though, what such a development in non-nuclear weapons would imply. The defence in a conventional war would not be compelled to concentrate its troops or use nuclear weapons if the attacking forces are strongly concentrated, but its deployment would still be dictated by the requirements not of conventional but of nuclear war. Mutual support would still be difficult to provide, and it would still prove equally difficult to prevent infiltration. On the other hand, guns of the envisaged type could dominate no-man's-land, cover the gaps between units and canalize penetrations. They would also make it unnecessary to mass artillery when concentrated fire-power is needed.

As a result the attacker would require a sizeable superiority in numbers and provide good targets for the new gun. While the

[1] 'Revolution on the Battlefield', *Daily Telegraph* (London), March 8, 1960, and reprinted in *Survival*, May/June 1960, Vol. 2, No. 3, p. 114.

necessary superiority may not be quite as high as in the last war, for the indicated reasons, it would probably have to be substantial.[1]

As it is, guns of this type are not with us, and the combination of bullet and spade, or shell and spade, can no longer crush any offensive. The attacker takes his protection with him, in the form of tanks, armoured personnel carriers and armoured guns, and the defence has not much additional protection because it must manoeuvre and move in the open almost as much as the enemy. Only the covering and holding forces will use the spade but sparingly so, because they must fulfil their function by manoeuvre. The shells of the defence artillery can no longer disturb the attacker's preparations, its fire-power has declined, and the attacker can count on better artillery support from his self-propelled guns. Mobile warfare militates against the spade, and dispersion and the expanse of the battlefield against the gun.

In a little-noticed address the then NATO Commander of Land Forces Central Europe, General Dr Hans Speidel, had this to say: 'It is no longer essential (in nuclear war) that the attacker has superiority over the defender—three or four to one was formerly considered desirable. Fire-power will make up the difference.'[2] If the defence adopts nuclear deployment in a conventional war, it is the decline of its own fire power and the increase in flexibility of the enemy's, coupled with the fact that both sides are almost equally exposed, which will make up the difference.

It must also not be overlooked in the calculation that the defence cannot indefinitely stay, or expect to stay, on the defensive; it must at some time wage, or be prepared to wage, a counter-offensive. To do so it requires some numerical superiority of forces in a war which it fights with conventional means. This aspect must not be forgotten if ever the question arises whether NATO can resist a specific conventional aggression with the conventional means at its disposal.

Are there, then, other deployment patterns which fulfil the necessary conditions, that is allow the defence to fight a conventional war in the conventional way, suit the requirement of nuclear war, and largely maintain the defence advantage over the attacker?

[1] At least as long as the attacker does not possess similar guns.
[2] 'Mission and Needs of NATO's Shield', *Army*, September 1960, Vol. II, No. 2, p. 34.

CONVENTIONAL WARFARE IN THE NUCLEAR AGE

The conventional deployment pattern, with its contracted battlefield, concentrated infantry, armour and artillery and, usually, static defence features, is so unsuitable for nuclear war that it cannot be adapted by way of modification. Insignificant static defences, coupled with nuclear deployment, would not influence the ratio of forces and large-scale constructions would be death traps if the conflict became nuclear. Usually psychological and political factors are also adduced against building fortifications. But could nuclear deployment be superimposed on conventional deployment?

Professor Kissinger suggests that the only safe way for conducting a conventional war against a nuclear power is to have a reserve in the combat zone deployed for nuclear operations. But this, he believes, would transform conventional war among nuclear powers into the most unstable kind of warfare because each side would be tempted to anticipate the other in the first use of nuclear weapons.[1] It is not obvious why this danger should be greater under this dual deployment system than it would be if all the troops had adopted nuclear deployment rules. However this may be, the dual deployment scheme seems hardly practicable. The conventional forces would have to be concentrated forward while the bulk of the nuclear reserve would be spread behind them and in great depth. Very considerable numbers of troops of all arms would be required. The losses among the conventionally deployed troops of the defence would be unacceptable if the attacker switched to nuclear war, and the presence of large numbers of these troops would make it difficult, if not impossible, for the defence to use nuclear weapons against the attacker who has broken through. But even if he has not done so, the conventional defence troops would have to be withdrawn once the attacker resorts to nuclear weapons. It is doubtful whether such a withdrawal would be at all possible, but if it succeeded the troops would block the roads and impede the movement of the nuclear defence reserves and their supply services; and if the attacker manages to follow on the heels of the conventional forces, he would be safe from nuclear attention by the defence while he himself could freely use his nuclear weapons against any target not too close by. It thus appears that a dual deployment scheme has little to commend it.

[1] *Nuclear Weapons and Foreign Policy*, p. 182.

DEPLOYMENT FOR CONVENTIONAL WAR

Would its usefulness be greater if the conventional forces acted as stay-behind parties? In this case they would not retreat and neither clog up the roads nor impede the use of nuclear weapons against the advancing attacker. But this would be a costly operation involving perhaps 12 divisions, neither selected nor armed and equipped for rear warfare, suddenly cut off from their land supply lines, operating in terrain not of their own choosing but where they happened to stay put, hampered by a great number of casualties caused by the enemy's nuclear weapons, and compelled to regroup and reorganize in an area where the enemy is strong. In the circumstances their employment as stay-behind parties would be a useless sacrifice.

It is obvious from the foregoing survey that there is no defensive deployment scheme which would fully satisfy the requirements of both conventional and nuclear war. Conventional deployment would invite nuclear disaster, nuclear deployment would deprive the defence of most of its traditional advantages, and if nuclear deployment is superimposed on conventional deployment, the defence would suffer from the disadvantages of conventional deployment, require a very substantial number of troops and weapons, and may find itself impeded in the use of nuclear weapons.

The attacker, as we have stated before, has an important advantage over the defence in this respect: the choice of weapons is his, and with it, often, the choice of deployment. He can decide on nuclear attack and deploy for nuclear warfare, without worrying about conventional requirements, while the defence must be prepared against nuclear as well as conventional attack. It is only when the attacker decides to wage a conventional war that he faces a somewhat similar dilemma since the defence might meet his attack with nuclear weapons. But even in this case he is favoured to a certain extent because he is aware that it depends on the weight of his attack whether NATO will respond with nuclear or conventional means. Having decided on the weight of attack he can deploy his forces accordingly.

He need not therefore switch from conventional to nuclear deployment while the defence might have to, and if it must switch it finds itself in a most difficult situation. As Marshal of the RAF Sir John Slessor has pointed out, 'for reasons less connected with tactics or training than with logistics and the organization of lines of communication and supply I do not believe a great army like Land Forces Central Europe could fight a conventional war from, say, D-day to D-plus-7 and then suddenly switch to a nuclear one'.[1] Indeed, a sudden switch from conventional to nuclear deployment might well overstrain the administration. Supply bases would have to be moved and dispersed, the formations in the field would have to take up new positions, different supply lines must be used, the railway trains and vehicles en route must be recalled or redirected, nuclear supplies would have to be brought forward, and all that on roads congested by the army's redeployment and in all likelihood subjected to enemy interference. The difficulties would not be much lessened if supplies were to a large extent moved by air. Such a massive reorganization would strain the supply services at any time; in the midst of battle it might lead to near-chaos.

NATO has recently decided to base its plan on a forward defence. In the circumstances this cannot, and it does not, imply that strong defence forces will fight the battle along the frontier of West Germany. The issue was clarified in an interview given by General Lemnitzer, the Supreme Commander, Allied Forces in Europe, when he stated that forward defence 'simply means that we intend to defend all allied territory in Europe. No area will remain uncovered ... The enemy would come into contact almost immediately with our covering forces. These contacts would help our commanders to determine where the enemy's principal attack was coming and to place the main defence forces on ground of our own choosing. Forward defence does not mean that we are going to conduct our main defence effort right at the Iron Curtain. But what has been accomplished during the last year does mean that the initial part of our mobile defence will be much closer to the Iron Curtain than has ever been possible in the history of NATO'.[2]

It follows from this statement that the forward defence zone will not be strongly manned and defended. Whether the rules of conventional or nuclear deployment will be observed for the main defence forces will in all likelihood be decided after the attack has been identified by the covering forces.

Militarily such a concept is not without its dangers if it means

[1] *What Price Coexistence?* (London, 1962; New York, 1961), p. 94.
[2] Interview with Dr Tom Margerison, *The Sunday Times*, October 6, 1963.

DEPLOYMENT FOR CONVENTIONAL WAR

that conventional deployment will be chosen if it appears that the conventional attack can be repelled with conventional means. Should the attack be at all serious, most of the defence forces would be committed to battle. It is at this point that the attacker can compel the defence to switch to nuclear deployment by one of the following means:

1. He has successfully deceived the defence about the weight of his conventional attack. He has a fine opportunity to unbalance the defence by starting a conventional war and inducing it to adopt conventional deployment; he can then raise the pressure, reinforce his troops, launch a major attack, compel the defence to make the possibly fatal switch to nuclear deployment during battle and overrun it before it has time to complete the redeployment and fight with nuclear weapons. Admittedly the attacker would take great risks—the defence might be able to redeploy in time—but he might think them worth taking.

2. The attacker wages a conventional offensive but concentrates only spearheads and keeps for the rest to the nuclear deployment pattern. If the attack thus masked appears to NATO to be only in the nature of a strong probe, NATO would decide to meet it in the conventional way. The attacker, having lured NATO into deploying its forces conventionally, might then suddenly introduce nuclear weapons and not only inflict great losses on his opponent but also compel him to redeploy under the most hazardous conditions.

There may be some who maintain that deception on such a scale will not be possible in either case. But those who assert so confidently that any massing or dispersing of enemy troops will be noticed should remember that Field Marshal von Rundstedt assembled a quarter of a million men and 1,000 tanks for his 1944 Ardennes offensive and, although the Allies had command of the air, he did so unnoticed. There are now, of course, additional reconnaissance means but there are also new devices for interfering with them.

It sometimes appears as if it were not sufficiently realized that the switch from conventional to nuclear deployment must be made by the defence before it can use nuclear weapons in a war that was hitherto conventional. The question usually asked is what advantage NATO will derive from introducing nuclear weapons after most of its shield forces have probably been overwhelmed already; it is tacitly assumed that the defence has always freedom of choice and can select the moment when to go over to nuclear war. The facts, as we have tried to show, are different. The switch to nuclear weapons entails a prior switch of deployment. A commander can redeploy his troops in comparative safety only once and that is before the main attack is made. In theory he can also do so at a later moment, viz. in the interval between battles, but he has no guarantee that there will be such an interval, and if there is it may be too late.

What conclusions can be drawn from the foregoing discussion?

These are the premises:

1. If the defence adopts *conventional* deployment—and a static defence system—in a conventional war, it needs only half as many forces as the attacker and possibly even less than that.

2. If the defence adopts *nuclear* deployment in a conventional war, it must be almost as strong numerically as the attacker.

3. If the defence is forced to switch from conventional to nuclear deployment during battle, it may become disorganized in the process.

It follows therefrom:

1. If the *attacker and* the *defence* deploy their troops *conventionally* for a conventional war, the defence requires smaller concentrations than the attacker to succeed.

   a. The attacker is therefore likely to suffer higher losses on the battlefield than the defence if the other side suddenly switches to nuclear attack.

   b. He also faces greater difficulties than the defence in switching from conventional to nuclear deployment since he must redeploy on a larger scale.

   c. He can avoid these disadvantages if he deploys for, and starts the war as, a nuclear war.

   d. He can maximize his advantages if he succeeds in inducing the defence to deploy conventionally while his main forces are deployed and ready for nuclear war. He then has little to fear if the defence initiates nuclear war and much to gain if he anticipates the defence and initiates nuclear war himself. The defence is then concentrated to a certain extent, thus providing him with useful nuclear targets, and must redeploy in the midst of battle.

   e. Conventional war and conventional deployment are only profitable for him if he either wants to gain very limited objectives or if he can overwhelm the defence before it has completed its redeployment; but his risk in the latter case is obvious.

2. If the *attacker* deploys his troops for *conventional* war and the *defence* for *nuclear* war, he is at a great disadvantage if the defence introduces tactical nuclear weapons.

3. If the *attacker* deploys his troops for *nuclear* war and the *defence* adopts *conventional* deployment rules he will hardly succeed in a conventional war. However, he has every chance to be successful if he initiates nuclear war.

4. If *both* sides deploy for *nuclear* war but fight with conventional weapons, the attacker has an advantage over the defence if he has numerical superiority. If tactical nuclear weapons are used the initial advantage is with the side that uses them first.

Hence we can draw the following conclusions:

The attacker in a war that may become nuclear has as a rule little to gain and much to lose if he chooses conventional deployment. He is more likely to succeed if he chooses nuclear deployment and fights with battlefield nuclear weapons right from the start.[1]

As for NATO, it wants to fight a war with conventional means as long as possible. However, it must adopt a deployment system that exposes it to the least risks, and it is obvious from the foregoing that it must elect nuclear deployment as its basic scheme. It must also bring up its numerical strength to almost that of the attacker if it wants to fight the war with conventional weapons only.

It is solely in this way that the defence can fight a conventional war and, when required, switch to nuclear war without having to redeploy on a significant scale. Right from the start of a conflict its forces will occupy the vast battlefield of nuclear dimensions and not the contracted one that was hitherto suitable for conventional war. The forces will be dispersed, not concentrated, there will be no continuous front or a succession of fortified positions distributed over the width and depth of the battlefield; the defence will mainly rely on mobile forces. The only static—or rather semi-static—element in the defence system will be supplied by the locally maintained militia.[2]

It is evident that the defence so deployed can effectively deal with concentrated forces of an attacker only if its reserves can

---

[1] He must, of course, consider the escalation risk.
[2] Cf. Chapter 3.

quickly be brought up to any danger point. They must either be air-lifted or be able to move under their own power on land at great speed. They must carry their supplies for several days and should be withdrawn as soon as their mission is accomplished.

But if the defence would bring up more and more reserves to the *front* it would soon find itself in a highly undesirable position: its forces would be dangerously concentrated. There is, as we said before, only one way to avoid this danger and that is to exploit the possibilities of the enemy's *rear* and send a portion of the troops there.

We shall try to find out in the next chapter how this can be done, and whether any rules can be established for the apportionment of troops as among the front, the enemy rear and our own rear.

CHAPTER 5

THE DISTRIBUTION OF TROOPS OVER THE FRONT AND REAR

THE previous discussion has brought out two points:
1. In a nuclear conflict the nuclear weapon is predominant and determines everything else: the deployment, the absence of static defence features, dispersal, and the extension of the battlefield. The entire concept of warfare is shaped by the nuclear weapon. It is, in Lt.-Colonel Miksche's words, the 'core around which the other arms must be grouped and to which they have to adapt themselves',[1] and so must strategy and tactics, organization and structure. This is common ground.
2. In a conventional conflict between nuclear powers, however, it is the *threat* of the nuclear weapon which determines everything else, and that again is the deployment, the absence of static defence features, dispersal, and the extension of the battlefield. But the core itself, the nuclear weapon, is absent; it does not, or not yet, enter into the contest, and we have no conventional weapon to substitute for it. The consequences have not yet been fully recognized.

The most important of these consequences is that the defence must be almost as strong numerically as the attacker. But there is an upper limit to the number of troops that can be accommodated on the battlefield, in our own territory, if nuclear deployment rules are observed. When this upper limit is reached it is impossible to say. It depends on two unknowns: the actual extent of the battlefield and in particular the number of troops employed by the enemy. *By upgrading warfare in enemy territory and allocating part of the forces to the enemy rear, the attacker as well as the defender can employ larger number of troops than it would be permissible if they restricted troop deployment to what has hitherto been regarded as their combat area, that is their own territory.*

But it would be wrong to think of rear warfare just as an expedient, devised to find space for an overspill of troops which cannot be squeezed into the battlefield and must therefore be

[1] *Atomic Weapons and Armies*, p. 146.

employed elsewhere. We have, in fact, already tried to analyse the reasons why the concept of rear warfare has become more attractive in a *nuclear* war: by distributing his striking forces over front and rear, the attacker can limit his troop concentrations for the offensive without reducing its weight.[1] The same observation holds true for the defender when he mounts his counter-offensive. The same verdict, for attacker and defender, applies in a *conventional* war under the nuclear threat. But that is not all. The attacker will carry the war as far into the defender's rear as he can. It is just as profitable for the defence to carry the war into the attacker's rear and fight part of the war in his territory. If the attacker can do it, so can the defence.

Warfare has always been dominated by conventions or patterns. How else can one explain that in previous centuries the opposing forces sought each other out, and then battle commenced? They had to do some seeking indeed because even large countries employed small forces hardly able to keep their frontier under observation, let alone defend it on a broad front. Unless fortresses commanded all the good routes, the armies, little dependent on supply lines, could have saved themselves much of the fighting if subtler means, such as Fifth Columns, had been more frequently employed. As it was, the issues were always settled on the battlefield. Sun Tzu's dictum, that 'supreme excellence consists in breaking the enemy's resistance without fighting', was seldom followed.

It is also striking that warfare procedures have not changed much over the years. There was always attack and defence. The attack was a frontal attack, or a flank attack, or a rear attack. If it was a frontal attack, it was carried out by attrition or by penetration while the aim of the flank attack was single or double envelopment. A rear attack, that is an attack originating in the rear, was relatively seldom carried out before the advent of aircraft because it required the presence of a force acting independently of the troops engaged in the main or holding battle.[2] And the defence has for long now adopted three forms: linear, area, and mobile defence.

We have accepted this demarcation line between attack and defence so completely that we never question it. The defence

[1] Cf. Chapter 2.
[2] Cf. for the above subdivisions Major-General J. F. C. Fuller, *The Second World War, 1939–45* (London, 1948), pp. 42–46.

does not, of course, stay permanently on the defensive: it executes a counter-push, or a counter-attack, or a counter-offensive, goes over to the offensive, and the erstwhile attacker and defender change their roles. But the dividing line between attacker and defender remains: each side is either the one or the other on any one battlefield. Neither side acted in both roles at the same time.

Besides this functional dividing line there is a geographical one represented by the fixed front. Apart from the isolated cases of rear attack, the attack started from the front. The territory behind each contestant was *his* territory and it was mostly left undisputed until and unless one side succeeded in breaking through. There were of course partisans in the enemy rear but their role was mainly to harass, not to engage in combat action, and World War II saw further extensions of warfare in the enemy rear, as we have mentioned before. It should be noted, though, that as far as these rear forces were combat troops, as distinct from harassing forces, they were as a rule used only to further the attack of the main force at the front; they were not used when their main force was on the defensive.

There are compelling reasons in modern war for seeking out the opponent and fighting it out with him. After Rommel's last successful push in the Desert he could have by-passed the British positions and marched on deep into Egypt but his supply lines would have been cut at once and his fate been sealed. He therefore had no choice but to attack at Alam Halfa. The practice of seeking out the enemy, unnecessary perhaps in olden times, must now be adhered to. But there is no need nowadays to respect the functional and geographical dividing lines.

It is probably correct to say that the essence of General Wingate's thoughts was to abolish both. He considered it the function of the Second Chindit Expedition, or Special Force in the official parlance, to engage in combat action, carried out in the enemy rear, and he wanted to attack with Special Force in the rear, regardless of whether the main force at the front was on the attack or the defensive.[1]

He went further than that. He no longer wanted the main

---

[1] Cf. Heilbrunn, *Warfare in the Enemy's Rear*, pp. 82 ff., 166 ff. Cf. for a similar concept Truong Chinh, *Primer for Revolt—The Communist Takeover in Viet-Nam*, New York 1963, pp. 181-2.

force to *push* back the enemy's front, as it was done in World War I; he wanted to *pull* it back, with Special Force, from the rear. This is the interpretation which must be given to his plan for the conquest of Siam and Indo-China. It was General MacArthur's island-hopping strategy translated into land warfare.

In his 'Appreciation of the Prospect of Exploiting Operation "Thursday"[1] of February 10, 1944' he advocated to take Bangkok and Hanoi by attacking the Japanese in the rear with the British main force; the British front forces were relegated to a very subsidiary role. He claims in that Appreciation that if Operation 'Thursday' succeeds in driving the Japanese out of Burma, the superiority of Long Range Penetration to normal formations in a normal operation will be clearly established, and normal divisions will no longer have any function in South-East Asia; they should instead be broken up into Airborne Long Range Penetration Brigades, Assault Brigades, and Airport-Garrison Brigades. He goes on to suggest that progress to Hanoi and Bangkok should be made by the use of Airborne Long Range Penetration Brigades which should build up behind them, at suitable distances, defended airports. Normal garrison troops should be stationed there, while the deeply penetrating Long Range Penetration columns would progressively force the Japanese to withdraw. The areas thus liberated were to be occupied by strong garrisons living in fortifications. The Long Range Penetration Brigades should operate around Strongholds.[2] General Wingate envisaged employing twenty to twenty-five Long Range Penetration Brigades, or about 100,000 infantry, in this campaign.

This plan was attacked at the time by all concerned, and nobody has come forward since to defend it. However, Field Marshal Sir Claude Auchinleck, then Commander-in-Chief in India, was prepared to further the expansion of Long Range Penetration troops if it was found necessary to use them for countering penetration into Assam by the enemy.[3] He too therefore realized that the British could fight their battle defensively at the front and offensively in the rear.[4]

[1] The code name for the Second Chindit Expedition.
[2] The Appreciation is reprinted in Major-General S. Woodburn Kirby, *The War Against Japan*, Vol. III (London and New York, 1961), Appendix 17, pp. 486 ff.
[3] Cf. Christopher Sykes, *Orde Wingate*, p. 459.
[4] The same concept was applied by General MacArthur for the Inchon landing. For the operations of 23rd British Infantry Brigade see pp. 145 ff. below.

It must be recognized that Soviet doctrine seems more inclined than that of the West to disregard the distinction between attack and defence, and also to regard warfare in their opponent's rear as well as in their own rear as a normal feature of future warfare. We have quoted the relevant references before; the statement by Colonel Baz bears repetition: 'For military science and the military leadership there arises the extremely complex task of correctly allocating the armed forces and military equipment for the conduct of combat at the front, for operations against the opponent's rear, and for the defence of one's own rear.'[1] This is the problem that we will discuss in the following paragraphs.

Three questions must be answered:

1. How many troops can be usefully employed, and maintained, in the enemy rear?

2. What should be the ratio of front troops to troops in the enemy rear?

3. How many troops are required for our own rear?

The number of troops that can usefully be employed in the enemy rear depends in the first place on the types of missions they are supposed to perform. We must then find out whether these tasks are indispensable and can only be performed by rear troops, or whether rear troops can perform them better, or more economically, than ground forces at the front or conventional missile artillery or the air force operating over enemy territory. We exclude reconnaissance tasks in the following survey because they require only relatively few men, their missions are as a rule of very limited duration, and they are really troops of the front to which they return after the execution of their mission.

Harassing missions and combat missions are, therefore, the two types of rear missions with which the following study is concerned.

Harassing missions, that is ambushing, mining, small-scale raiding, sabotaging, kidnapping, disrupting supply lines etc., will be performed by the British SAS, the United States Special Force, and partisans. The SAS whose operations include reconnaissance, ambushes, sabotage, raids on nuclear

---

[1] 'The Characteristics of Modern War', *Survival*, November/December 1959. p, 191; and, under the title 'Soviet Military Science on the Character of Contemporary War', in Garthoff, *The Soviet Image of Future War*, p. 97.

targets and headquarters, kidnapping, and creating alarm and despondency, frequently works on its own but may also temporarily join forces with partisans. SAS parties are up to fifty strong. They, like the Special Force, operate in the far rear. The Special Force, however, almost always works together with partisans. Its units usually consist of teams of two officers and ten men with the mission to form, organize, train and direct a guerrilla detachment of up to 1,500 men.[1]

Partisans operate in the near and far rear. They have harassing and also combat assignments. In an international war—as distinct from a revolutionary war, uprising or civil war—their activities are co-ordinated with those of the front troops. The recognized categories of co-ordination between guerrilla and regular warfare are, according to Mao Tse-tung, in strategy, in campaigns, and in battles.[2]

As far as co-ordination in strategy is concerned, we have had no experience of it in Europe: in the last war there was no co-ordination between the Red Army and partisans on that level, and Tito's activities in Yugoslavia were mostly of an independent character. We must turn to the Far East and Mao's theoretical exposition for enlightenment. 'In co-ordinating with the regular army', he says, 'the guerrillas not only play the role of strategic defensive at the present moment (May 1938) when the enemy is launching a strategic offensive, and will not only handicap the enemy defence when the enemy concludes his strategic offensive and turns to defend the areas he has occupied, but will also repulse the enemy forces and recover all the lost territories when the regular army launches a strategic counter-offensive.' Since it was only 'through the cumulative effect of many offensive campaigns and battles in both regular and guerrilla warfare'[3] that the Japanese could be defeated, some form of co-ordination in strategy between the two forms of warfare was required. In a European conflict guerrilla warfare is unlikely to play a similar role in the strategic concept of either side, and there is little point in discussing practical examples.

There is a decisive difference between this type of co-ordination and co-ordination in campaigns which imposes on the

[1] For a detailed discussion, cf. the Index references in Heilbrunn, *Warfare in the Enemy's Rear*.
[2] Cf. Mao's 'Strategic Problems in the Anti-Japanese Guerrilla War', in *Selected Works of Mao Tse-tung*, Vol. II (London, 1954), pp. 132-134.
[3] Ibid., p. 125.

guerilla leaders the duty, in Mao's words, to 'take positive action against the enemy's most vital and most vulnerable points so that (the guerillas) may succeed in crippling and containing the enemy, disrupting his transport and raising the spirits of our own armies engaged in interior line campaigns'. The most outstanding demonstration of this type of co-ordination was given by General Giap, the Viet-minh commander in the war against the French Union forces, in the Dien Bien Phu and the winter/spring campaigns 1953/54. 'They were', as Giap states, 'most successful models of co-ordination between mobile warfare and guerilla warfare, between the face-to-face battlefield and the theatres of operation in the enemy's rear, between the main battlefield and the co-ordinated battlefields all over the country'.[1] These co-ordinated battlefields were far apart and far away from the main battlefield: in the Red River Delta, South Central Viet-Nam, Lower Laos, Middle Laos, and the Western Highlands. By suddenly appearing there in some strength, the Viet-minh rear forces of guerillas, semi-regulars and militia drew off the French Union Forces into all directions and kept them tied down in areas of Giap's choice. He thus not only forestalled a French offensive but also made it virtually impossible for them substantially to reinforce or relieve their troops at Dien Bien Phu, or to gain undisputed possession of the vital Red River Delta. At the same time he was assured that his troops would maintain their local superiority throughout the battle for Dien Bien Phu. He neatly summed up his strategic concept: 'in addition to the units which have to be *scattered* in order to *wear out* the enemy, it is necessary to regroup big armed forces in favourable conditions in order to achieve *supremacy* in attack at a given point and at a given time to *annihilate* the enemy.'[2]

There are a number of other examples of co-ordination in campaigns. In General Wingate's Ethopian campaign in 1941 indigenous partisans supported the regulars throughout and finally, reinforced by some regulars, blocked the Italian escape route before Agibar, while Wingate's forces pressed the enemy from the other side against the partisans and obtained his

[1] General Vo Nguyên Giap, *People's War, People's Army* (New York, 1962), pp. 109–10.
[2] Ibid., p. 104; italics supplied. Cf. also General Vo Nguyên Giap, 'Inside the Viet-minh', in Lt.-Colonel T. N. Greene (ed.), *The Guerrilla—And How to Fight Him* (New York, 1962), p. 155.

surrender.[1] In the Soviet summer offensive of 1944, the partisans had the task of slowing down the German retreat after the Red Army had reached the Dnieper; they forced the Germans on to a limited number of roads and railways which they blocked until the Red Army had moved up and could annihilate its opponent.[2] Also in 1944, with the Allied invasion of France, the Resistance in the country carried out a number of specific tasks which it had been assigned under four sets of plans: the Green Plan for railway sabotage, the Violet Plan for sabotage to telephonic and telegraphic communications, the Blue Plan for sabotage to electric power stations, and the Tortoise Plan for blocking roads. While co-ordination was successfully carried out in all these campaigns, Chinese attempts to co-ordinate the front and rear effort in the Korean War ended in failure.

Co-ordination in battle is concerned with two types of rear activity: the rear forces either harass the enemy, or join in combat together with the front by engaging him in his rear. Most partisan movements, stationed in close vicinity to the main battlefield, have done the first and, in the last war, particularly the Soviet partisans and the French maquis have carried out the latter task for short periods.[3]

The general objectives of rear warfare discussed so far are threefold: to deprive the enemy of reinforcements, arms, equipment and supplies; to drain his manpower; and exceptionally, to give direct combat support to the front. The objectives, time, place, type and intensity of the rear operations are co-ordinated with the requirements of the front. The rear efforts are in all cases subsidiary to those of the front troops. These rear forces do not make the main effort; they do not disorganize the enemy; their mission is to make a contribution towards this aim.

While the partisans will again carry out harassing missions in a future war, the regular forces which will be allocated to the enemy rear will have combat assignments. These troops will, of course, also harass the enemy to some extent: they will interfere with his communications and supplies, raid special targets, ambush and mine. However, the main task of the regular forces

---

[1] Cf. W. E. D. Allen, 'Gideon Force', in Irwin R. Blacker, *Irregulars, Partisans, Guerrillas* (New York, 1954), p. 385.

[2] Cf. Major Edgar M. Howell, *The Soviet Partisan Movement, 1941–44* (Washington 1956), p. 196.

[3] Cf., for examples, Heilbrunn, *Warfare in the Enemy's Rear*, pp. 102, 107–8, 139 and 149.

THE DISTRIBUTION OF TROOPS

operating in the rear is to carry the fight into the enemy's territory and engage him there in combat.

What can we learn from the precedents?

Two types of operations must be considered, namely those of ground troops who, after breaking through the enemy front or moving round his flank, continue the fight in the rear and secondly, those of air-landing troops and Special Forces who after infiltrating by land, sea or air, engage the enemy in his rear.

Generally speaking, these troops had either strategic or tactical functions, they either directly participated in the main battle or they carried out independent missions, and their effort was either the main effort or a subsidiary one. The following examples may serve as illustrations.

I. Strategic employment of troops in the rear.

(a) participating in the main battle. In this case the rear is the theatre in which the decisive effort is made. The Schlieffen Plan, designed for Germany's conduct of World War I, provided that the massed right wing of the German Army in the West should execute a wheeling movement hinged upon Diedenhofen-Metz, sweep through Belgium and, after clearing Northern France of the enemy, press him back against his fortress belt along the French-German frontier from Verdun to Belfort; the French, compelled to fight with their front reversed, would then be totally defeated. The decision would be sought in the rear.

Similarly, the second, unexecuted phase of the Manstein Plan for the defeat of the French and British armies in World War II envisaged that they should be enveloped in the rear of the Maginot Line, again with their front reversed, and again, the decision would be sought in the rear.

(b) fighting independently. The classic example is provided by the descent of a German airborne corps on Crete in 1941 where it opened a new battlefield. The success of the whole operation was dependent on the success of the airborne assault. It achieved its objective though the losses were heavy.

II. Tactical employment of troops in the rear.

(a) participating in the main battle. The forces in the rear can make either the main or a subsidiary effort. During Rommel's advance in the Desert Campaign his mobile forces, working their way from the front to the rear, were meant to make the decisive effort while the positional forces at the front were mainly employed in a holding role. On the other hand the Allied airborne forces at Arnhem and the Rhine crossing made a subsidiary effort; the main role in the advance was played by the ground troops. There are, however, cases where front and rear play an equal part: the German victories in the great encirclement battles of the Russian campaign were won by like contributions from the front and rear.

(b) fighting independently. This was at times the mission of the Second Chindit Expedition.

The partisans stayed in the last war continuously in the rear, from the inception of their movement to the liberation of their area; their main task was to harass. The combat troops, on the other hand, usually fought only for short periods in the rear. However, Tito's regular forces, by far the largest element of his 'National Liberation Army and Partisan detachments', were engaged in combat almost continuously from 1941 to 1945, and General Wingate had intended that the Chindits should operate for extended periods. It is obvious that the war in the enemy rear can be effectively conducted on the scale required in the future only if the forces in the rear have the capability to stay and fight there for long periods.

The partisans owe their power of survival and operating effectiveness to the suitability of the chosen terrain and the support of the population. They can therefore melt into the countryside and are thereby helped by their inconspicuousness—they wear civilian clothes and conceal their arms—, their command of the local language, their familiarity with the local customs, and often their local domicile and employment. The nature of the terrain makes it not only possible for the partisans to disappear from sight, it also prevents the enemy from using his transport, heavy weapons and equipment. The population provides the partisans with intelligence about the enemy's movements and intentions as well as likely targets for their own operations. Finally, because the enemy is restricted in the use of many modern weapons, they can carry on the fight with a minimum of supplies, especially as they usually live on the country.

Combat forces sent into the enemy rear will have few of these advantages. In particular, they must be as well armed and equipped, as a rule, as the enemy whom they are likely to meet.

Tito's main force, the National Liberation Army, was regarded by him as a force of regulars, and the Germans on the spot paid him the compliment of agreeing with him. His regular troops survived, and were able to fight effectively, because they were favoured by the terrain, increasing popular support, a constant stream of new recruits, and Allied support. Their leadership was equal to that of their opponents and their devotion to duty higher than that of some of the occupation troops. It also helped them that their mobility was superior and that the occupation troops, who also had to guard the coast-line against an Allied invasion and fight Mihailovitch's guerrillas, could not mass the required superiority against the dispersed National Liberation Army's units and the partisans attached to them or operating near their homes. As it was, Tito's regular elements had all the advantages of partisans and few of the disadvantages of a uniformed force of regulars, fighting in alien country, possibly against strong forces of all arms.

The question how uniformed forces can maintain themselves in enemy territory for a lengthy period never arose in World War I and was little discussed in World War II or, for that matter, afterwards. In the first half of 1942, Staff planners of the British Eighth Army, then fighting in the Desert Campaign, examined a scheme of this nature, the so-called 'cow-pat' scheme. 'This was the term given to establishing a series of supply bases one by one in front of our present positions. Strong armoured forces were to be based on these administrative areas, and they in turn would be protected by infantry and artillery. The idea was to force the enemy to attack us, as he could not go on ignoring these thrusts into his territory. It had a fundamental weakness, and that was that it automatically made us disperse our forces, whilst it gave the enemy the opportunity of concentrating against these detachments.'[1] The idea was therefore never put into practice.

A more fruitful and imaginative attempt at a solution of the problem was made by General Wingate. He recognized the strong points of long-range penetration and the advantage it would confer on the side which employed troops deep in enemy territory. He also realized that the weak point in any such scheme was the vulnerability of the forces in the rear, due to

[1] Major-General Sir Francis de Guingand, *Operation Victory* (London, 1947), pp. 108–9.

their likely numerical inferiority and their lack of heavy arms and equipment.

General Wingate had taken a hard look at the practical results of the short-range penetration tactics applied in Malaya and Burma by the Japanese who, in suitable terrain, had infantry precede the main body by as much as seven days. These advance parties had set up road blocks in the British rear, delivered surprise attacks on reinforcements and, generally, attacked where their opponent was neither prepared nor able to fight. Since supporting arms are of little value in broken and forested areas, the maintenance problem did not loom large; the advance parties received their supplies when they made contact with their main forces.

The advent of aircraft and wireless, General Wingate pointed out, had made long-range penetration possible; this form of penetration, he stated, influences not only the enemy's forward troops but his whole military machine and his main plan; the attack is directed against targets which in the nature of things he is unable to protect—lines of communication, reinforcements, headquarters, aerodromes, rest camps and so on. 'To use a prize-fighting parallel, in the forward areas the enemy's fists are to be found, and to strike there is not of great value. In the back areas are his unprotected kidneys, his midriff, his throat and other vulnerable points'.[1] The enemy, General Wingate held, could protect himself against these rear attacks only by withdrawing troops from the front, and the British main force was prepared to take advantage of this situation.

General Wingate realized that deep penetration was not possible everywhere. The penetration forces must be concentrated in order to strike a blow, to move over long distances, to receive supplies by air, and to fight their way out if the enemy surrounds them. Hence, he argued, the columns can only operate where either the terrain is favourable, or where the enemy is thin on the ground and a great number of warlike inhabitants can and do support the columns.

In order to provide the Chindits with the means to hold on, General Wingate based their operations on a system of strongholds. These strongholds were to be defended to the last. They had a number of purposes: they were an asylum for the wounded, a magazine for stores, a centre of administration for

[1] *Training Notes by Major-General Orde Wingate, Commanding LRP Forces*, no date.

local inhabitants, a base for supporting aircraft, a defended airstrip and, above all, an impregnable fortress. 'We wish', he stated, 'firstly to encounter the enemy in the open and preferably in ambushes laid by us, and secondly to induce him to attack us only in our defended Strongholds'.[1]

The strongholds had to be located in areas inaccessible to enemy wheeled transport, artillery and tanks. They had to rely on earthworks and minefields for immediate defence and provide for co-ordinated fire of its weapons. They received tactical air support. They were also secured by floater companies and floater columns outside, which would harass and attack the enemy if he advanced against the strongholds. Such floater units had already been used successfully before by 4 Corps in Burma where each garrison had satellite mobile columns, hidden in the jungle outside the defended areas and ready to pounce on the rear of an attacking enemy.[2]

The Chindits, being lightly armed, were mobile, and their mobility provided them, in General Wingate's concept, with another advantage: they could move away from the enemy into country into which he would be afraid or unable to follow: the jungle would serve the Chindits as a screen.

If we look on the map at the possible north European battlefields and the enemy lines of communication, we must conclude that there are few possibilities for adopting or adapting the stronghold concept. Even if air support were assured—and this is a big If—there would be no need for an enemy to bring up large forces of infantry, tanks or artillery in order to deal with strongholds. He can direct missile fire against them from a great distance. Inaccessibility is therefore no longer a sufficient protection, nor can earthworks, mines and floater columns in future improve the stronghold's prospect against an enemy equipped with missile artillery. Furthermore, the Chindits' air supply lines were never seriously disturbed by the Japanese because the Allies had air superiority; they will hardly have this advantage in a European theatre deep in the enemy rear. The supply lines of long-range penetration forces will be as vulnerable as those of

---

[1] 'Special Force Commander's Training Note No. 8—The Stronghold', issued February 27, 1944, reprinted in Brigadier Michael Calvert, *Prisoners of Hope* (London, 1952), pp. 274 ff.
[2] Cf. Field Marshal Viscount Slim, *Defeat Into Victory* (London, 1956; New York, 1961), p. 220; Kirby, op. cit., p. 171, and Sykes, *Orde Wingate*, p. 497.

the enemy. Only small forces and guerrillas have a chance of survival in the areas in question.

Could the Chindit concept be applied in northern Europe without the backing of strongholds? The answer is in the negative. The stronghold was meant to assure, as much as possible, local superiority to a numerically inferior force. Without the stronghold it cannot exist for long in the deep rear as the Chindits experienced after they left the strongholds and moved north towards the Japanese main force on the front. Even though such rear forces could now take heavier arms and equipment along, the enemy in northern Europe would still be superior on both counts.

There will be rear warfare, as it was understood in World War II, in any future war: SAS, Royal Marine Commandos, Rangers, the United States Special Force, air-landing troops and, as we said before, partisans will all play their part, and so will Chindit-type forces in suitable country.[1] But large-scale attacks will not originate in the deep rear—possibly apart from rare strategic air-landings—: they will have their starting point behind the contact line and will be carried on from there, over continuous areas over which the rear troops will gain control.

What is the operational aim of these rear troops?

They will pull back the enemy front.

They achieve this aim by launching an offensive, directed at:

1. Isolating the battlefield by

(a) blocking the approach routes of enemy reserves to the battlefield;

(b) cutting the enemy supply lines to the battlefield;

(c) eliminating special targets;

2. Co-operating in the single or double envelopment of enemy troops caught in the areas between front and rear troops.

They carry out these missions regardless of whether their own front troops are retreating, holding on, counter-attacking or waging an offensive.

Since large-scale air-landings would be extremely risky and many small-scale widely dispersed landings ineffective, the approach routes of the main body of the rear forces to their battle areas will be overland. Some air-landing troops will precede, accompany, or follow them in order to facilitate their advance; they will seize key objectives on the axis of advance in

---

[1] Cf. Heilbrunn, *Warfare in the Enemy's Rear*, throughout.

THE DISTRIBUTION OF TROOPS

the near rear where the main body can quickly join up with them.

The rear troops must have ground supply lines, at least as an alternative to air supply routes, because of the uncertainties of air supplies in the exposed enemy rear. Overland supply routes are also required for heavy arms and equipment which the rear troops need for the execution of their missions.

They will go in after the enemy's first-line troops have joined battle with the opposing front troops and are therefore largely tied down elsewhere.

The rear objectives will be allocated as follows:

1. The ground forces will carry out the main combat missions.

2. Airborne troops, including airborne armour, will gain favourable positions for attack or deprive the enemy of a favourable position for counter-attack; gain a bridge or road or a railway section, or deny them to the enemy for reinforcements or retreat; or remove an obstacle in the way of the advancing troops, such as batteries or strong-points, or launch a surprise attack on an enemy held position. All targets are located in the near rear.

3. Special Forces will deal with important targets, mostly in the far rear.

The ground forces are composed of tank forces, armoured infantry, and support troops. Their theatre of operations is across the rear of the enemy or friendly main advance routes, that is opposite the main battlefield which they expand into the enemy rear by their operations. The battlefield thus gains a new dimension. Operations are therefore not confined to the area west of the Iron Curtain—where the front troops try to push back or hold an attacker—but also take place behind it—where the rear forces pull him back.

This extended battlefield must retain its cohesion; otherwise front and rear troops could not effectively conduct combined operations with a maximum of forces in dispersed order. The rear forces must therefore shift their theatre when the enemy moves, and they must shift it in the direction in which he moves. If he advances and their own side retreats they must follow him, and if he retreats and their own side advances they must move deeper into enemy-held territory. Only by fighting the enemy in front and rear in this manner is it possible to obtain local

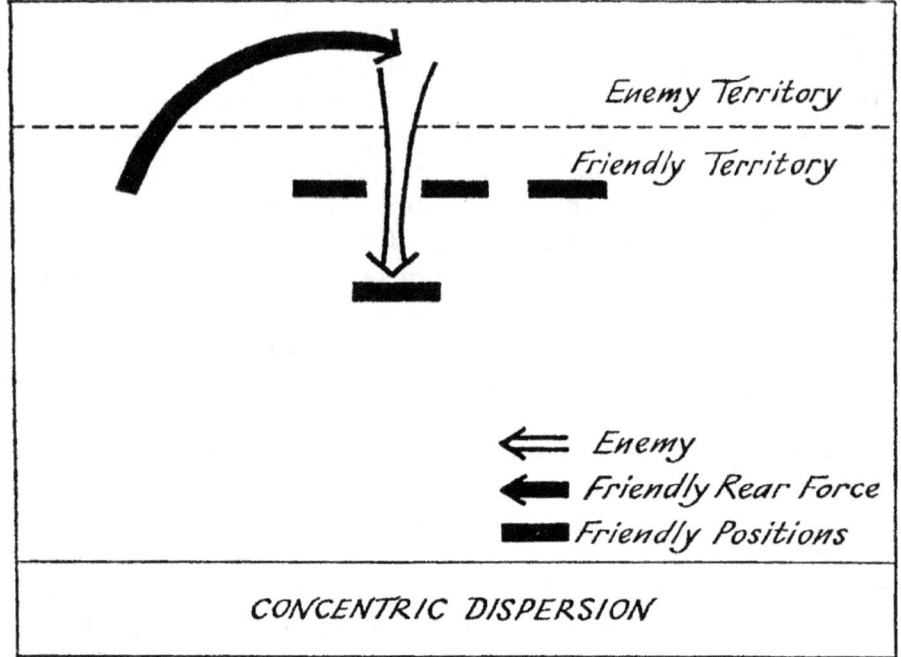

CONCENTRIC DISPERSION

superiority without concentrations and to confront an enemy with strength in dispersal. Only in this way can a number of battle groups strike jointly without concentrating. Above all, only in this way can dispersed forces fight successfully against a concentrated enemy *without resorting to nuclear weapons*. The enemy is in the centre of their ring: their deployment is concentric but they do not concentrate.

If it is the recognized purpose of the rear forces to make this *concept of concentric dispersion* possible, larger formations should be sent on a mission far away in the enemy rear in order to fight it out there only if some specific task of importance calls for and justifies such an enterprise. And we need not contemplate, as has been done in the United States, whether in the future an airborne corps will be able to land several hundred miles beyond the already established battleground, then fight its way right down the enemy communication lines and thrust its combat power into the backs of an enemy already fighting in another direction. The rear troops should not fight in the far rear[1] or advance from there to the near rear where they would arrive at

[1] Cf. Heilbrunn, op. cit., pp. 165 ff.

THE DISTRIBUTION OF TROOPS

an uncertain time and with their strength considerably reduced by their contacts with the enemy. They should instead take advantage of the new opportunities: while the enemy's striking force will be concentrated, his formations left behind will be dispersed and their front symbolic. Under such conditions the penetration of the 'front' from the contact line to a considerable depth can much more easily be effected than hitherto, and the rear forces, proceeding on the ground, can take their heavy arms and equipment with them and keep their supply lines open. At the same time the hitherto thinly held forward area must be strengthened.

The aim of the rear operation, as stated before, is to pull back the enemy. By attacking the enemy's striking force from the rear and holding back his reserves and supplies on the ground and in the rear, the rear forces cut the life line of the enemy's striking force and besiege him on the battlefield. If the siege can be maintained, the enemy's fate is sealed.

It would be wrong, however, to conclude that the main task of the rear forces is to cut off the life line, and that rear attacks on the enemy's striking forces will be only secondary missions. In practice the distinction between primary and secondary missions will be less clearly marked because, by cutting into the enemy rear, the force lays itself open to counter-attacks from all sides by the enemy's striking elements, his reserves, and his troops allocated to rear defence. The troops sent into the enemy rear cannot select their opponent; they will have to fight against all comers.

It must also not be overlooked that, because the new battlefield must retain its cohesion with the already established one and the ground on which the rear forces fight changes constantly, the type of enemy forces they are likely to meet changes too. In those circumstances they may often not be able to choose whether to fight primarily against enemy front or rear troops.

Generally speaking it may be more important at times that the forces in the enemy rear assist in the counter-attack on the enemy striking force or take upon themselves some of the weight of the enemy attack, and at other times that they prevent it from being sustained by incoming enemy reserves and supplies. And sometimes both tasks may be of equal importance.

It may be held that the rules developed here do not really differ from accepted practice. It is, of course, true that every envelopment isolates the battlefield, and it is equally true that in the Desert battles both sides tried to move round the enemy's flank into his rear as often as they could. However, the special features of the concept of concentric dispersion should not be overlooked. They are:

1. In the past there was usually a clear-cut distinction between attack and defence. Troops were either attacking or on the defensive. It is suggested here that this distinction should in future, in a conventional war against a nuclear power, no longer be maintained, and even if the front is on the defensive, the rear must attack.

2. Whenever the attacker decided in the past to carry out an enveloping movement he had the initiative,[1] and he assigned to his front troops the role they were to play in the forthcoming operation. Here the attack in the rear is carried out even if, and especially when, the opponent holds the initiative.

3. A review of the various campaigns of World War II and especially World War I shows that the enemy was not very often attacked in his rear. It is suggested here that rear attack should be a regular feature of *every* battle.

The role suggested for the rear forces cuts right through the hitherto recognized categories which we mentioned before. It can be strategic or tactical, and the rear forces may participate in the main battle, fight independently, or do both at the same time.

On the correct appreciation of the needs and the likely strength of the opposition depends the required strength of the rear forces and, consequently, the proper apportionment of forces as between front and rear.

As many troops can be employed in the enemy rear as at the front if the rear theatre can be sufficiently extended. It seems unlikely that even the most ardent supporter of rear warfare will suggest that the allocation of forces to the rear should be higher than to the front. Because the potentialities of this type of rear war have never been tested, the rear allocation will in all likelihood be smaller, and that assessment seems entirely appropriate as long as the requirements stated in the previous paragraph are observed. That the rear forces are indispensable for the tasks earmarked here is obvious; they can only be performed by rear troops. The air force will and can assist but it cannot go it alone

---

[1] The Inchon landing was a rare exception to the rule.

instead; it would be unrealistic to expect that it could isolate the battlefield in a future war with conventional means; nor can it thrust as much sustained conventional combat power into the rear of the enemy striking forces as properly equipped ground troops can. Nor can conventional missile artillery fulfil the tasks of the rear forces; it can only support them.

How can the Special Forces and partisans help the regular rear force? Their main theatre would not be the battlefield itself but the areas further to the rear, and they can assist in much the same way as they did in the last war and in Indo-China. They will raid, ambush and harass, pay special attention to the lines of communication, they will tie up enemy forces by their activities, and they will supply Intelligence.

As far as partisan operations are concerned, it has often been pointed out that the terrain must be favourable, the population must be friendly and it must have an aptitude for guerrilla warfare. While in parts of Germany—and beyond—the terrain is favourable, it is widely held that the Germans would not do well as partisans.

This view seems to have gained support because the German Army deprecated the idea of the people in arms, and also because Germany's effort at the end of the last war, in the form of the *Werwolf* guerrillas for the defence of the alpine redoubt, collapsed so completely. But the reaction of the Army and the people was only natural: the German Army met partisans in the last war usually as opponents, that is as 'bandits', and not as helpers, that is as 'patriots', and even where the Germans found partisan support, as happened in parts of Russia, their experience was not always happy. And the German people, exhausted after six years of war, were in no mood to put up any final and utterly hopeless resistance in the Alps.

Yet it is of some importance to know whether German partisans could be expected to play a part in other circumstances, that is in an East-West conflict. A German author, Hellmuth Rentsch, has investigated the question when a population can be considered adept at partisan warfare, and finds the answer in tradition and character of the people.[1] Tradition, he states, is most prevalent in mountain and tribal populations. As far as the people's character is concerned he argues that the mountain population is more warlike than the plainsman, and highly

[1] *Partisanenkampf, Erfahrungen und Lehren* (Frankfurt am Main, 1961), pp. 51 ff.

civilized peoples and the urban population are less suited to partisan warfare than are the more primitive peoples and peasants. There are nations, he contends, which are inclined towards revolution, conspiracy and rebellion, and others which respect order and authority. 'The Germans are inclined towards order at any price', and this would make them unsuitable for partisan war. But it appears that Mr Rentsch thinks primarily in terms of revolutionary wars, not international wars when patriotism is the motivation and tradition a useful attribute to the successful conduct of partisan operations.

The Germans have a greater tradition in irregular warfare than it is widely supposed. The evidence for this tradition is to be found in the peculiar form of the German freecorps which go back to the Napoleonic wars and were inspired by the example of the Spanish guerrilleros. These German irregular corps, formed and led by serving or retired officers and composed of volunteers and regular soldiers, took up arms against Napoleon while their monarchs remained irresolute and inactive. Neither friend nor foe treated them as soldiers: After Major von Schill, one of the freecorps leaders, and his officers had been captured by the French, they found them guilty of 'robbery with violence on the open highways and of entry into inhabited houses by the use of force or ladders', and the King of Prussia refused to rehabilitate these officers even after Napoleon's final defeat.[1] Freecorps of a somewhat different character were formed even earlier, often by students who rose spontaneously to fight small wars against intruders, such as the Freiburg volunteers who took up arms in the seventeenth century against the French invaders. The Academic Legion in Munich and the Students' Corps in Kiel took to arms in 1848.[2] After the First World War a great number of freecorps came into existence. Former officers formed large or small units of volunteers, mostly veterans, peasants' sons and unemployed, and they were joined by university and high school students when the Prussian socialist government called for support. Some of these freecorps had republican, others right-wing tendencies, yet all gave more or less loyal support to the government, if only because they shared its internal and

---

[1] 'Der Kampf und Untergang des Schillschen Korps', in *Deutscher Soldatenkalender* 1959, Siebentes Jahrbuch, München-Lochhausen, p. 93.

[2] Generalmajor Dr Walther Grosse, 'Aus der Geschichte des deutschen Freikorps', ibid., p. 131.

THE DISTRIBUTION OF TROOPS

external enemies, that is the left-wing extremists at home and Poles and Russians in the east.[1] When the Reichswehr came into being later on, many of the freecorps were taken over and formed its nucleus.

What all these freecorps had in common was their determination to fight for a cause, and to do so with their own resources and without the backing of a regular army. They were irregular forces of volunteers engaged as a rule in small warfare. They were akin in spirit and resolve to partisans.

What is more, Germany found in World War I an outstanding guerilla leader who has often been called the German Lawrence. His name was Wassmuss, his post that of German consul to the Persian Gulf, his area of operations was there, and his aim was to incite the Persians to revolt against the British. Britain and Russia had in 1907 signed a convention which divided Persia into two spheres of influence, a British and a Russian one. When World War I started, Wassmuss hoped that a revolt would induce the British to divert large numbers of troops to Persia. Due to his own part in the affair his expectations were fulfilled.[2]

Already before the outbreak of war he had gained the esteem of sheikhs and tribesmen. He wore Persian dress, he spoke high Persian as well as the local dialect, and he was an accomplished horseman.

He rode out to the tribes in the Gulf hinterland, had talks with headmen and officers of the gendarmerie, and they agreed to gather their men at a sign he would give them. In May 1915 the sheikhs were summoned to a conference at Borazjan; the tribesmen were committed to war. In the words of Christopher Sykes, 'Persian neutrality could be maintained only by the unnatural presence of British and Russian troops on Persian territory. So long as these troops remained passive the Persian Government would never declare war on the Allies. The aim of the Germans was to provoke the British and the Russians to abandon their passivity.'[3]

There were a few skirmishes at first, then the tribesmen rose and attacked the British garrison at Bushire. At the same time a German expedition—not under Wassmuss—made its way

[1] Cf. Harold J. Gordon, *Die Reichswehr und die Weimarer Republik, 1919–1926* (Frankfurt am Main, 1959), pp. 32 ff.
[2] Cf. for the following, Christopher Sykes, *Wassmuss, 'The German Lawrence'*, (London, 1936).
[3] Ibid., p. 115.

through Persia towards Afghanistan with the intention of provoking a rising there on the border with India; the British and Russians therefore formed a cordon on the border of Persia with Afghanistan. In Wassmuss's territory the battle of Dilbar took place, there were further raids, followed by the second battle of Bushire. For a time the campaign proceeded more leisurely—Wassmuss was constantly moving about, exhorting the chiefs and trying to smooth over tribal differences—and then it gathered pace again; battles and engagements, some of them bloody, were fought at Deh Sheikh, Khaneh Zinian, Ahmadabad, outside Shiraz and at Firuzabad. In October 1918 the revolt collapsed. Persia had not declared war, yet Wassmuss had achieved much: Christopher Sykes credits him with being in some measure responsible for the British surrender at Kut,[1] and so did the Kaiser.[2]

In World War II Persia, Afghanistan and India figured again in projects of Admiral Canaris's Counter-Intelligence Organization and Himmler's Reich's Main Security Office. Attempts by men of Skorzeny's Special Formation at inciting Persian mountain tribes to revolt soon ended in failure, and equally short-lived were German hopes of promoting revolution in India with the help of Subhas Chandra Bose. Just as there was no successor to Lawrence on the Allied side, so Wassmuss's performance was never equalled by any other German. But many small-scale actions by members of the Brandenburg Division, the German 'Commandos' of the last war, serve to underline the fact that the German capabilities for partisan-type operations are of a high standard, and German history confirms this finding.

That the French maquis can be relied on to give a good account of themselves was shown in the last war and requires no further discussion.

Whether and how far partisan movements should be prepared beforehand are questions of considerable importance; they have been discussed elsewhere.[3] It would be useful to second Special Forces on the American model to partisan areas. The Special Force would take charge of the operations of partisans as well as of troops which have been overrun, so that their activities could be co-ordinated among themselves and with the requirements of the front and of other rear forces.

[1] Ibid., p. 143.   [2] Ibid., p. 164.
[3] Cf. Heilbrunn, *Partisan Warfare*, pp. 115 ff.

THE DISTRIBUTION OF TROOPS

How many troops are needed for securing our own rear? We have already mentioned in Chapter 3 the missions of the German and French territorial defence units: to secure the operational bases of the NATO units, to give them logistical support and, in France, to take care of partisan tasks. In particular these units ensure the security of the lines of communication, protect airfields, prevent sabotage and other subversive activities, fight against disloyal bands and assist in fighting enemy air landing troops and enemy penetration on the ground, they also lay emergency bridges, keep designated military roads clear for troop movements, assist the troops in the use of the telephonic and telegraphic facilities, provide the troops with transport, and look after POW's.[1] They will exchange liaison teams with NATO units in order to ensure close co-operation. Their area of sole responsibility starts from the rear boundary of the combat zone and extends over the entire communication zone, while responsibility within the combat zone is divided. Intelligence for NATO should be added to their functions.

It is obvious that the total unit strength of 50,000, envisaged for Germany by 1966, will be sufficient only if the fight against larger enemy penetrations by air and on the ground is immediately taken up by NATO troops and the territorial defence units are only required in this context in order to raise the alarm and provide technical assistance, such as scouts, transport and communications. If the territorial defence units are supposed to deal with these intrusions themselves or make a major contribution, their strength must be greatly increased; otherwise NATO forces must be strong enough in the communication zone to do the job. The latter is preferable because the defence units are not under direct control of the NATO commanders.

There are, of course, NATO troops, viz. reserves, in the communication zone. Their tasks would be twofold: to be available as reinforcements on the battlefield and to fight against significant enemy penetrations in the rear. The reserves will be comparatively large to fulfil the first function. As Captain Liddell Hart has stated, war experience shows that the higher the ratio of mobile reserves to the troops holding the more forward posi-

---

[1] Cf. for the above, Oberst Emil Schuler, 'Zusammenarbeit französischer Streitkräfte mit deutschen territorialen Dienststellen', *Revue Militaire Générale*, December 1962, pp. 644 ff.; and by the same author, 'Landesverteidgung in der Bundesrepublik', ibid., March 1963, pp. 322 ff. Also Messmer, loc. cit.

tions, the better it is, and he suggests that half the available forces should be held as mobile reserves, not tied to a particular sector.[1] If the reserves are to take on the second function as well, that is to engage enemy forces in our own rear, some increase in their strength seems desirable, yet not at the expense of the troops in the more forward positions but by providing additional NATO divisions.

If, say, six NATO divisions were available in a sector likely to be attacked, two divisions should be placed in the more forward positions, three be held as reserves, and one dispatched to the enemy rear. While the distribution of troops over front, our own and the enemy rear cannot be determined beforehand with any degree of exactitude but must always remain flexible, the suggested allocation might serve as an indication of the basic strategic requirements in the various areas. Front and either rear will draw on the reserves when necessary.

How does Soviet military doctrine compare with the above? We have seen before that Russian planners expect war in their own rear and intend to conduct large-scale operations in the opponent's rear. They have made no statement about the ratio of forces to be allocated to the front and the rears. They think of frequent employment of airborne troops whose task it is to carry the attack forward; they are apparently the first or rather the most advanced wave of the attack. To pull back the opposing front is not a specified mission of theirs, and once again the difference in postures between East and West must be taken into consideration: because Soviet military strategy, now as in the past, is basically conceived in terms of attack, the main task of their rear forces may well be to advance further into the enemy rear, while the West, standing on the defensive, is primarily interested in holding an attack and, hence, it should use rear forces for pulling back the opposing front to its start line.

Soviet special airborne troops, which we mentioned in Chapter 2, will carry out missions similar to those of the SAS. Partisan tasks and operations are not discussed in the openly published literature. In some countries of the NATO Alliance the threat from partisans with alien loyalties may be serious, but not so in Germany; she is, however, exposed to the danger of sabotage by East Germans in West German uniform or plain clothes.

---

[1] *Deterrent or Defence*, pp. 171–2.

CHAPTER 6

TECHNICAL PROBLEMS OF CONVENTIONAL WARFARE

'THE art of achieving a rapid and decisive victory over the enemy with the minimum losses to personnel and equipment requires continuous and inquisitive search for armaments, better organization of tactical groupings, and reliable methods of administrative support. The one able to solve these problems in peace-time will have greater expectations for success in war'.

This is a sound appreciation, by a Soviet colonel, of the technical problems of warfare,[1] but a qualification should be made in respect of logistics. 'Previously', says Major W. H. Pope, 'logistics could be treated as an afterthought . . . We could always develop our tactical doctrines and plans first and then decide what logistic support would be required . . . It is essential to note that the capability of the nuclear weapons to destroy an area totally forces us to consider logistics at the same time as we consider tactics . . . It is useless, indeed it is downright harmful, to talk of mechanization *until* the logistic problems of nuclear war have been solved.'[2] Although this statement refers to nuclear war, it is equally applicable to a conventional war between nuclear powers.

We have seen that the troops in such a war must be deployed as if they were fighting a nuclear war, mainly for two reasons: only in this way can the risks to one's own side be minimized if the opponent introduces nuclear weapons, and only in this way can a large-scale and possibly fatal shift from conventional to nuclear deployment be avoided if and when either side switches to nuclear war.

Likewise, it would be almost impossible to change the organization and structure of the army in the field, if a conventional

[1] Lt.-Colonel K. Leonov, 'Logistics and Supply of the Soviet Army: USSR', translated by Major Gavrisheff, US Army Reserve, first printed in *Military Review* and reprinted in *Canadian Army Journal*, July 1959, Vol. xiii, No. 3, p. 110.
[2] Major W. H. Pope, 'Problems of Future War: The Tactical Doctrine and Organization Required by Land Forces', *Canadian Army Journal*, April 1959, Vol. xiii, No. 2, p. 49.

war became nuclear. The structure and organization for nuclear war must be so designed as to be also suitable for a conventional war.

What, then, are the structural and organizational requirements for nuclear war, what are they for conventional war, and what adjustments, if any, are necessary to fit them for both types of war?

The structure and organization of the NATO forces were at first designed for a nuclear conflict. They have not been standardized but they have all one characteristic in common: the fighting units are organized below divisional level into battle groups which are small enough to minimize the effect of enemy nuclear weapons yet still powerful enough to conduct independent operations effectively. As a result the division has been split up into self-contained combat units, and the divisional headquarters is responsible for general tactical control, support and supplies of the battle groups.

The British, West German and French forces conform to the triangular arrangement of three brigades per division; one of the three British divisions, though, has only two brigades, while the other two are composed of two British plus one Canadian brigade and three British brigades respectively.[1] The divisions of these three countries are predominantly of two types: they are armoured or infantry divisions. The Bundeswehr also has an airborne and a mountain division. The armoured divisions have usually two armoured and one infantry brigade, while the infantry divisions are composed of one armoured and two infantry brigades, the latter consisting of a tank battalion, an artillery battalion, and three infantry battalions some of which may be armoured. Each brigade—or the smaller battle group of infantry, a tank battalion and support troops—is self-contained and can operate independently for a period.

The American forces also used to adhere to the standard pattern of armoured and infantry divisions. They introduced the pentagonal system under which the infantry division was composed of five battle groups, mostly infantry, of about 1,400 men plus one battalion each for engineering, signalling, ordnance, two artillery battalions, one tank battalion, a cavalry squadron and medical and transportation services. The pentagonal struc-

[1] The British Divisions will possibly be reorganized in the near future and then consist of two brigades each.

ture was originally adopted because it seemed to allow best for dispersion and all-round defence—three to attack, one to hold and one to defend, as Brigadier Michael Calvert once expressed it.

But with the needs of conventional war in mind, the American planners have been seeking further to improve the flexibility of their NATO divisions and recently introduced the ROAD system which discards to some extent the rigid dividing line between armoured and infantry divisions and replaces them by a kind of standard division. The new system also abolishes the pentagonal structure. The ROAD division consists of a divisional and three brigade headquarters with five to fifteen battalions—usually about eleven battalions—altogether. The battalions are of one or more of the basic types, armoured, infantry, armoured infantry, and airborne. There is in addition the divisional echelon, mainly consisting of an air component, three howitzer and two artillery battalions, with altogether 6,500 men.[1] The precise effect of the ROAD scheme is difficult to assess since it depends on the availability and right admixture of units for each particular mission. But the scheme makes it possible to have armour and infantry under their own headquarters and, alternatively, to form mixed brigades, or battle groups, as the situation demands.

It has always been a matter of contention whether the three-brigade system or the pentagonal one is preferable in a conventional war between nuclear powers. The United States has now decided that there is nothing magic in the figure five, that the troika brigade system has worked well in past conventional wars and should be retained, and that the new system makes sufficient allowance for nuclear war.

It has long been recognized that in conventional war integrated units below division-size can often play a useful part. The Germans, it is true, kept the division as the smallest mixed formation throughout World War II. However, on the Allied side the need for much smaller units was already felt in 1942. In that year the British formed the first battle groups of less than divisional size in the Desert campaign. In 1944 they formed brigade groups and the Americans regimental combat teams. The quicker movement of units required that decisions be made at

[1] Cf. Neville Brown, 'The Armies in Central Europe', *RUSIJ*, November 1963, Vol. CVIII, No. 632, p. 346.

lower level than hitherto, and increased striking capabilities of integrated teams made co-ordination at that lower level possible. 'The effect of the nuclear weapon has been to force this intimate co-operation to an even lower level.'[1]

Evidently, the structure must be shaped after the role of the troops. Their role is

1. In nuclear war to conduct purely mobile operations aimed at forcing the enemy into concentrations, to annihilate him with nuclear weapons and exploit nuclear strikes. They must control their territory and themselves avoid concentrating as far as possible.

2. In conventional war to conduct purely mobile operations aimed at closing in and capturing or destroying the enemy with conventional means. They usually do not want their enemy to form concentrations. They must control their territory—to hold it would mean reverting to static warfare—and themselves avoid concentrating as far as possible.

The differences between the nuclear and conventional roles are, of course, due to the presence or absence of nuclear weapons. In a conventional war, and especially a mobile one, the infantry must rely on the support of tanks, artillery and aircraft. The previously described organization, with its co-ordination at a lower level, is therefore suitable for conventional operations if it gives the infantry the support it needs, and also assures the armour of sufficient infantry support.

In the first place, tanks are needed because the enemy has them. The belief that tanks are obsolete is, in Captain Liddell Hart's words, 'at least dubious, and could be very precarious for any army which discards tanks to fight the enemy's tanks, in favour of guided missiles'.[2] General von Mellenthin expresses himself more forcefully: 'Armoured units of the highest mobility will play the decisive part in nuclear war', and 'ground forces without strong armour have no future in wars of tomorrow.'[3]

The capability of tanks to survive in a conventional war depends in the first place, naturally, on how well the enemy is

---

[1] Major W. H. Pope, op. cit., p. 51.
[2] *Deterrent or Defence*, p. 187.
[3] Major-General F. W. von Mellenthin, 'Armor in the Atomic Age', *Ordnance*, July/August 1960, reprinted in *Canadian Army Journal*, Summer 1960, Vol. xiv, No. 3, pp. 55 and 59. Also optimistic for the future of tanks is Richard M. Ogorkiewicz, 'Missiles Against Armor', *Marine Corps Gazette*, January 1959, Vol. 43, No. 1 p. 55.

equipped with anti-tank devices in the particular sector and how well they are sited and operated. If his anti-tank front is strong, the tanks' chance of survival gradually diminishes the closer they come to the enemy's short range weapons. As long as the armour is exposed only to the enemy's longer-range weapons, it can as a rule effectively deal with them; its fire-power is probably sufficient for this purpose, though it will find the enemy's positions better concealed and harder to hit than hitherto.[1] However, in the final 100 or 200 yards of the assault it is unlikely, as Major N. A. Shackleton has pointed out, that the armour can accompany the infantry because the enemy will have numerous short-range anti-tank weapons, and it will be necessary for the infantry first to clear the intervening ground of anti-tank launchers before the tanks can move in.[2] But if their own side is on the defensive, they will have an even better chance, and certainly a better one than the enemy's armour, because they operate in their own territory.

It has often been said that the quality of tank design will in the end decide whether the tank or the anti-tank weapon will be superior. Speed, manoeuvrability, fire-power and weight of armour as well as silhouette are still decisive factors. Plastic materials may replace part of the armour, there may be some new form of propulsion, and rocket-firing armour might play a special role in dealing with anti-tank missile nests. It could well happen again, as it did in the last war, that at times the tank and at others the anti-tank weapon will be dominant.

If, then, the tank still has its function on the conventional battlefield, the present ROAD system offers great advantages. The composition of the enemy's forces, the commander's intentions, and the nature of the objective and the terrain decide what the proportion of armour and infantry should be, and the very flexibility of the ROAD division makes it possible to attack with formations mixed accordingly, while it also allows adherence to the customary defensive pattern in which the infantry division was required to hold ground and the armoured division to counter-attack.

Much of the infantry must, in fact, be armoured too. 'Modern infantry cannot live on the battlefield without the armoured

---

[1] Cf. Major N. A. Shackleton, 'Anti-Tank Weapons and their Influence in Battle', *Canadian Army Journal*, Summer 1961, Vol. xv, No. 3, p. 38.
[2] Ibid., p. 38.

personnel carrier—a protective vehicle designed to carry infantry across country, under heavy fire, to within striking distance of the enemy.'[1] Infantry without APCs can too easily be separated from its accompanying tanks. It will have to dismount at a distance from the contact line in order not to expose its own carriers and also to deal with the enemy's anti-tank weapons. It may seem paradoxical that the infantry must leave its protective shells just when it apparently needs them most but this is not truly so. Only in APCs will the infantry be able to keep close contact with the tanks and pass safely over the intervening ground until it comes close to the contact line; without the protection of the APCs it would not be available to clear the last 200 yards or so, dismounted, for the tanks. Armoured infantry is equally indispensable in defence against an attack by enemy armoured infantry. However, supply problems may limit the use of APCs. 'Until we can develop a logistical system that can supply and maintain a completely mechanized field force despite nuclear interdiction, then the infantry must remain on its feet', states Major Pope,[2] and while supplies will be less subject to dislocation in a conventional war, restrictions on the use of APCs may at times be unavoidable.

In view of the logistical problems of modern war light infantry certainly has its advantages. Captain Liddell Hart has proposed to use it for policing and mobile defence. 'They would be completely capable of moving off the roads—but not through mechanization. Their cross-country capacity would come from lightness of equipment. They would be armed mainly with light weapons that a man can carry, and only such supporting weapons as can be carried on a mule'.[3] Similarly Marshal of the Royal Air Force Sir John Slessor demands that 'we must restore the mobility of the boot ... and drastically reduce the enormous quantities of motor transport (and fuel to keep it moving) which in fact is such a drag on the mobility of modern armies.'[4] Desirable as the achievement of these aims would be, it is difficult to believe that such formations could move with the necessary speed over the enormous distances of the modern battlefield and survive on the battlefield. The Korean experience, it is true,

---

[1] Lt.-Colonel Alun Gwynne Jones, 'Lack of Infantry the Crucial Weakness'. *The Times* (London), October 17, 1963.
[2] Op. cit., p. 50.
[3] *Deterrent or Defence*, p. 65.
[4] *The Great Deterrent*, p. 282.

makes clear that light infantry cannot be dispensed with altogether, but the remedy is not to deprive infantry of its APCs but to make it dismount where necessary.

Conventional forces will need, of course, all the artillery support they can get. It would be well, as we mentioned before, if the guns could be developed which the artillery presently lacks, viz. a gun with a range of up to 30 miles and a weapon similar in mass effect to the atomic weapon but without its undesirable characteristics. There would be little purpose in discussing the composition of the divisional artillery of the various NATO forces. The fact is that at present the Red Army has an advantage in divisional and independent artillery, and it is therefore to be welcomed that the US will increase its divisional artillery by 17 per cent[1] at a time when British medium artillery seems to be declining.

If the artillery shortages are made good where they exist, it is hardly to be feared that the present integrated formations below divisional level are too small to fight conventionally. The present brigades are almost of the same size as the various combat groups of the last war, and where there are now battalion groups they can easily be brought together and function as a brigade for a more compact effort. If, on the other hand, they operate as battalion groups, they are not so small as to be exposed to piecemeal destruction. Once it is recognized that the ground forces, in nuclear and conventional war alike, must be dispersed and conduct purely mobile operations, it becomes obvious that one and the same structural pattern can be suitable for both types of war, and particularly the ROAD system seems to fulfil this requirement.

The West is confident that it can gain air superiority in the areas of its choice. It must be added, though, that it will take longer to achieve and be less profitable when attained than hitherto. As Mr Neville Brown rightly remarks, in view of the vertical and short take-off and landing techniques, command of the air can no longer be gained by crippling a limited number of large airfields, and the 'growing power and flexibility of land-based anti-aircraft defences is making it less and less easy to turn (it) to decisive advantage'.[2] But without air superiority the ground troops have only a limited chance to achieve their objectives.

[1] Neville Brown, 'The Armies in Central Europe', p. 346.
[2] *Strategic Mobility*, p. 193.

Army aviation of the major NATO forces—mostly consisting of light observation, liaison and transport aircraft and helicopters—is integrated at divisional or brigade level[1] and sometimes at corps level.[2] Generally speaking, any system that is good enough in those fields for the requirements of nuclear war will also fulfil the needs in conventional warfare. The needs are, however, different where tactical air support is concerned; conventional forces look to the air force in this respect to a very much greater extent than troops in nuclear war. These aircraft should not be organic but under the control of the theatre commander who alone can make the necessary allocations;[3] the Air Force is represented in his headquarters, to advise him.

The role of airborne troops in a future European war is very much in doubt at the present time. That troops can still be dropped and landed in their own territory is generally accepted but there seems to be little chance of dropping paratroops over enemy-held territory, the reason being that the transport aircraft must fly during the air-drop at a height at which they are extremely vulnerable to the enemy air defences. However, a new method of landing troops without using parachutes is being tried out by the US Air Force. The soldiers will sit in so-called people pallets which hold 12, 24 or 48 men. These pallets will be carried on the open cargo ramp at the rear end of low-flying assault aircraft and dropped from heights up to 35 feet; they then slide along to the ground for about 100 feet. It is claimed that one air squadron could drop 3,000 men in less than six hours.[4]

Helicopters, flying at low heights, are also immune to enemy radar devices and rockets but their low speed makes them extremely vulnerable otherwise. It is, however, held that they could fly troops and equipment and land them, or drop the equipment, a few miles behind the enemy lines. The Soviets seem to regard helicopters as the main means of landing tactical airborne troops[5] while transport planes will be used by them for operational landings.

---

[1] Cf. Brown, 'The Armies in Central Europe', *RUSIJ*, pp. 344, 345, 346 and 347.
[2] Bundesministerium für Verteidigung, *Die Heftreihe Unser Heer*, Heft 3, *Heeresflieger* (Hamburg, 1962), p. 6.
[3] Major W. H. Pope, loc. cit., p. 54.
[4] Cf. 'Troops to land without using Parachutes', from the Aeronautical Correspondent, *The Times* (London), July 23, 1963.
[5] Sokolovsky, p. 292.

The success of such operations depends on the strength of the opposition and the chances of silencing it. We must probably accept the fact that as far as the enemy rear is concerned, paratroops can in future be employed only in small operations of the commando type, that is to say in *coups de main*, that helicopter landings are restricted to areas within a few miles behind the contact line, and that landings deeper in the rear by fixed wing aircraft require local air superiority and support by missile artillery and air-mechanized cavalry, as Colonel Parson has suggested,[1] and air cover may be needed for the period of the ground operation. Unless the area of the landing ground has been thoroughly reconnoitred in advance, larger operations of this type, even if carried out with contour flying aircraft, must be considered extremely hazardous. Where they are worth while, on the axis of advance, an enemy will be strong and the attrition rate high enough to jeopardize the mission, and where he is weak the objective will often not warrant the risks.

If one takes into account that overland infiltration is now considerably simplified by the absence of a fixed front and the dispersion of the ground troops, only two types of airborne operations seem worth while in the future, namely the already mentioned commando operations, particularly against special targets, and strategic landings at the beginning of a war for the seizure of strategic positions on a global basis.[2] There may be scope for operations of a third—Chindit—type, designed to tie down the enemy rear security forces and launched against his periphery. Otherwise helicopters and transport aircraft had better remain reserved for transport duty within the confines of the territory held by our own forces, including those who have been dispatched overland into the enemy rear, as suggested in Chapter 5.

Aircraft are the most genuine dual purpose weapon at present available;[3] their load can be conventional or nuclear. But, as we mentioned before, this versatility has also a great disadvantage: the opponent can never be sure how they are armed, and the appearance over the front of aircraft carrying conventional weapons may be the signal for the enemy to start a nuclear war

---

[1] *Missiles and the Revolution in Warfare*, p. 117.
[2] 'Romulus', 'Future Employment of Airborne Forces', *RUSIJ*, May 1955, Vol. 100, No. 598, p. 239.
[3] Strachey, op. cit., p. 110.

in the mistaken belief that a nuclear attack upon himself is imminent. Their usefulness is therefore seriously restricted in a conventional conflict.

There are, or can be developed, other dual purpose weapons, viz. guns, howitzers, rockets and missiles. But the dual-purpose attribute is somewhat misleading: these weapons are often either too cumbersome or too expensive to be used conventionally. It is therefore hardly correct to assume that the troops in the field can fight both types of war because they have dual purpose weapons with them. What makes the dual usefulness of tactical weapons even more doubtful is the fact that one single atomic gun can do the work of 35,000 field guns of medium calibre[1] while the same gun, firing a conventional weapon, would just be one in a crowd. There seems little point, then, in bothering with tactical all-purpose weapons. What is more, the same argument that is used against 'all-purpose' aircraft applies here too: if the enemy observes preparations for firing the weapon, he might think that a nuclear warhead is about to be launched against him, even if it is in fact only a conventional one, and a nuclear war might be unleashed by mistake. This fact cancels out any advantages which could possibly be claimed for dual purpose ground weapons.

It is not thought that the Russians have dual purpose weapons. It seems that their conventional rocket launchers are organic to divisions while nuclear tactical weapons and large rockets are operated by an independent branch of the armed forces. In the NATO formations, battlefield nuclear weapons are usually integrated at divisional and also at corps level. Whether the integrated or the independent system is preferable is a question which concerns the nuclear war organization and is therefore outside the scope of this study. It need only be pointed out here that in a conventional war, or in the conventional phase of a war, the troops in the field should not be handicapped by having to guard and move the more cumbersome nuclear weapons of the divisions and lower formations with them and that a separate organization would therefore be more suitable. However, since a war might start as a nuclear one or become nuclear later on at any unpredictable moment, the requirements of nuclear war must here obviously override those of a conventional conflict.

[1] Miksche, *Atomic Weapons and Armies*, p. 112.

TECHNICAL PROBLEMS OF CONVENTIONAL WARFARE

Bacteriological and chemical warfare are also outside our scope. There has been remarkably little discussion of these topics, compared with nuclear warfare, although the importance and impact of those types of war could be as great as those of a nuclear confrontation. Organizationally the bacteriological and chemical defence companies, whose job it is to reconnoitre, test, warn, treat and decontaminate, are divisional troops and the battalions are corps troops. This allocation is equally suitable for conventional and nuclear war. Whether these troops would possibly also be charged with waging these forms of warfare has not been made known.

Regardless of whether one subscribes to the concept of controlled dispersion or of concentric dispersion, it is obvious that the effectiveness of dispersed formations in mobile warfare depends to a large extent on the effectiveness of the communication system. The Hobart plan, adopted by the British Army of the Rhine, introduces a new concept of battlefield communications.[1] Hitherto communications in battle were tied to the chain of command and the headquarters organizations, each with its own signal system; under the new system which will be introduced over a period of ten years, a flexible network is superimposed upon an operational area, any number of units and formations can introduce their radio system into the network at any point, and the signal centres can move freely without losing contact with each other. Thus even small sections can have their own communications and can be effectively controlled. The value of this system, in nuclear as well as conventional war, is obvious.

The greatest danger to the smooth working of any communication system threatens from jamming by the enemy. The attacker works to a plan, and as long as everything goes according to plan, he will be less affected by jamming in the initial stage than the defender who must reconnoitre, receive reports, come to a decision and transmit orders and who therefore depends largely on the smooth working of the communications. Another hazard arises if the opponent manages to monitor the messages or to transmit faked reports and orders over the system, a sometimes very much more effective activity than the interruption of communications.

[1] We follow here the report from the Defence Correspondent 'Army Communications to be Reorganized', *The Times* (London), September 7, 1962.

As for training, says General Gale, 'our armies must be trained both for decisive and speedy intervention in conventional modern war and also for taking part with tactical nuclear weapons in a general war.'[1] He also emphasizes the need for troops to be trained to move by transport aircraft and helicopter at a moment's notice, and to carry out mobile and active patrolling to cover the gaps between units. 'The necessity for cross-country mobility will lead to increased demands on specialist training for drivers and wireless operators'.[2] If it is accepted that nuclear war and conventional war against a nuclear power are both characterized by important identical features—dispersion of troops, purely mobile warfare, absence of a front line and vastness of the battlefield—training for both types of war is not as difficult to give and absorb as it is sometimes imagined. There is, of course, the well-known difference: in nuclear war the troops support the weapon, in conventional war the weapons support the troops. This means in tactical or operational terms, admittedly somewhat simplified, that the troops force the enemy to concentrate in nuclear war and to disperse in conventional war, and few training problems should arise in this context. It also means that different techniques of infantry and tank co-operation with guns are required—again, these skills can be acquired—and finally, that troops must be able to handle conventional and nuclear battlefield weapons. If it is remembered how easily many of the last-war partisans learned to use any weapon, however unfamiliar, that fell into their hands, and to do so without manuals and instructions, the weapon training of troops should not present any major difficulties either. Generally speaking, even in a nuclear war troops will be required to fight frequently without nuclear support and training for nuclear war includes much training for conventional war anyway.

There is one sphere, though, in which training of a special kind is necessary, for conventional as well as nuclear war, and that is training for fighting in the enemy rear. Field Marshal Viscount Slim, the reader will remember, has stated that if troops are cut off from their land communications with their bases, 'the main problem is apt to be the question of maintaining the right morale'. The morale problem is of similar importance

---

[1] General Sir Richard N. Gale, 'The Training of Land Forces', p. 605.
[2] Ibid., p. 607.

for troops fighting behind the lines, even if their supply lines remain intact. Rear warfare requires a special mentality of officers and men, and it can be acquired by training. This training does not only take in marching and digging and patrolling and signalling; it aims, above all, at getting the minds attuned to the hazards and mystics of rear warfare.

If there is any training problem it may well be of a different nature: in the small regular British Army troops must be able to fight any kind of war: the irregular, the conventional, the nuclear war, on the battlefields of Malaya, Kenya, Cyprus as well as in Central Europe and elsewhere. It speaks for the versatility of the British soldier and the ability of those responsible for training and organization that General Sir John Hackett can say that 'on transfer from operations of this sort (viz. irregular warfare) to a NATO assignment these battalions lost no time in reactivating those parts of their structure which had been permitted a temporary atrophy. This transition, well prepared at either end of the cycle, was usually quite smooth and . . . it was quite quickly made'.[1] However, there are limits to the 'One Army' concept which even the best of training cannot overcome if there is too much of it for too many and too varied types of operations. On the available evidence it appears that these limits have not yet been reached.

We have stressed at the beginning of this chapter that, contrary to the past, tactical doctrines can in future no longer be determined without reference to logistical capabilities.

Logistical support of the various NATO forces is a national responsibility. 'The consequence is that each national contingent could at present fight at only a limited distance from its own bases, and the NATO forces as a whole can reap very few of the advantages of mobility with which their equipment is endowing them'.[2] Yet progress towards unification has been painfully slow and attempts at weapons standardization have been frequently unsuccessful.

There is no point in going into details; they are well enough known, as it is, and that goes in particular for weapons standardization. As far as the unification of the logistic systems is

---

[1] General Hackett, op. cit., p. 8.
[2] Institute for Strategic Studies, Adelphi Papers, No. 4, *The Defence of Western Europe* (London, May 1963), p. 11. POL supplies are integrated. In wartime NATO can only re-allocate supplies in the combat zone.

concerned, any attempt in this direction should be welcomed. The Institute for Strategic Studies in London has recently been critical of a logistic tie-up between the United States and Germany because the American logistic system is held, for reasons of distance, to be more complex than is required for the European countries.[1] This argument, however, does not seem to take sufficiently into account that in a war, be it nuclear or conventional, West Germany will be so exposed that her production is bound to be interrupted and she must rely on overseas, and that means mainly American, supplies. A unification of the two logistic systems could therefore be only advantageous, and other NATO member countries might follow this lead. Also desirable would be a scheme that avoids the present crossing of communication lines but it must be recognized that this would involve a reorganization of NATO which would present great difficulties.

The individual logistic systems are comparatively unchanged from those of the last war; they still rely on fixed depots, linked by road and rail with the forward area, on wheeled vehicles with limited cross-country performance, and on bulk fuel tankers away from the network of steel pipelines.[2] The depots, roads and railways are particularly endangered; they offer an easy target to the enemy and the roads may be congested by refugees and evacuees. Colonel Smallman therefore rightly underlines the need for vertical and short-take-off aircraft, permanently assigned to the logistic service; they permit the redeployment of stocks and help to lighten the load on ground transport. Ground movement must be improved by vehicles with greater cross-country capabilities—the possibilities of hovercraft (air-cushioned vehicles) have not yet been fully exploited—and it can, as Colonel Smallman suggests, to some extent be shortened by augmenting the steel pipelines with plastic ones extending as far forward as possible.[3] Most depots are at present not far enough forward, but, again, this is a matter of some complexity.

The storage requirements are determined by estimates of the probable duration of a conventional conflict, and here British and German appreciations differ from the American ones. The

---

[1] Ibid., p. 11.
[2] Colonel W. A. Smallman, 'Mobility and Logistics', *Revue Militaire Générale*, March 1960, p. 295.
[3] Ibid., pp. 299 ff.

TECHNICAL PROBLEMS OF CONVENTIONAL WARFARE

British and German planners hold that a battle in western Europe will be fought conventionally only for a limited period after which the losing side will use tactical nuclear weapons, followed by strategic nuclear weapons if negotiations do not take place in the meanwhile, and 30 days' stores of supplies and ammunition are considered adequate in the circumstances. The Americans believe that the West is capable of fighting a conventional battle for a longer period and that operations in Europe should be planned on the basis of 90 days' stocks. In view of the latest estimates of Soviet strength[1] there is much to be said for the American standpoint, especially if Captain Liddell Hart's calculations are accepted.[2] According to this authority NATO needs 26 mobile divisions to keep 40 Soviet divisions in check; these 26 divisions would be sufficient to satisfy 'the force and space conditions', that is to say they would provide a 2 to 3 ratio of forces and could hold the front, and the required number of divisions would be even less if there was a citizen militia, which France and Germany are now about to set up. Within a month of an outbreak NATO would have about 35 divisions plus the territorial defence forces while the Soviets would have about 65 divisions. If allowance is made for the greater number of combat soldiers in a US division, the 2 to 3 ratio would still be maintained after 30 days, and in this view a conventional conflict, in which the other Warsaw Pact forces do not take part, could therefore last longer than that, especially if further Soviet reinforcements can be cut off.

Much has been said in recent years about the need for austerity in administrative support, and western troops have been the subject of some criticism. Lt.-Colonel Miksche has stated that 'in order to maintain one NATO type division of 15000–18,000 men in the front line, some 32,000 men are needed in the rear area. With the same money and manpower the Soviet Union would form not 1 but 3 divisions'.[3] The Soviet armoured division is part of an overall slice of 20,000, the Bundeswehr will have 29,000 soldiers per divisional slice and the US pentomic division has 43,000. But, as Mr Neville Brown points out, it must not be overlooked that a number of factors account for these discrepancies. Among them are Soviet reliance on railways rather than

---
[1] Cf. the Introduction to this book.
[2] In *Deterrent or Defence*, p. 172. We do not share this view; cf. Chapter 4.
[3] *The Failure of Atomic Strategy*, p. 49.

roads for supplies, the greater number of riflemen in an American, compared with a Soviet, division and, as far as Germany is concerned, a lower level of logistic and other forms of support than is usual in the us Army.[1]

The list of desirable logistic improvements is long enough as it is: unification of supply systems, weapons' standardization, a larger allocation of aircraft and cross-country vehicles, an increase of stores above the thirty days' level, erection of more forward depots, and disentanglement of supply lines. Mobile operations, dispersed formations, and an extensive battlefield all make for high demands on the logistical service, and they are still further increased because supplies have to be kept in, and delivered from, dispersed depots. Thus the degree of mobility and dispersion of the troops in the field is geared to, if not governed by, the capabilities of the supply service. So are staying power, sustained combat effectiveness and responsiveness of the units to command. It also largely depends on the flexibility of the supply service whether the switch from conventional to nuclear war can be successfully carried out.

Preferential attention should therefore be given to the state of the supply service.

---

[1] 'The Armies in Central Europe', pp. 342 and 344.

CHAPTER 7

THE SWITCH FROM CONVENTIONAL TO NUCLEAR WAR

We have tried to show in the preceding chapter that it cannot be predicted, with any degree of accuracy, for how long NATO can fight a war conventionally. Not only the respective strength of the forces enters the calculation but also the state of their armament and the quality of their supply service. NATO may be able to fight conventionally for more than 30 days, but it might be less than that especially if a surprise attack inflicted considerable losses on its forces. However this may be, it would not be wise to fix a time limit and state that NATO will fight with nuclear means after its expiry: an ultimatum of this sort might only invite the opponent to anticipate the date and throw the first nuclear punch himself.

There are eight principal reasons which could induce NATO to continue a hitherto conventional war with nuclear means:

1. It believes that the enemy is about to use nuclear weapons and forestalls him;

2. Its losses in men, weapons and equipment during the conventional fighting are such that it cannot successfully fight the war with conventional means;

3. It has been pressed back beyond a certain geographical line and cannot hope to regain the lost territory with conventional means or resist successfully if its freedom of manoeuvre is still further reduced;

4. Its troops in the field, its communication network or supply service have been dislocated to such an extent that only nuclear means will give it the respite necessary for reorganization.

5. The conventional phase has dragged on for so long that NATO must bring the war to a quick end, especially because its production, shipping, and the morale of the population do not stand up any longer to the demands of a protracted war.

6. The use of small nuclear weapons is considered to bring the

enemy to the conference table because it has now been brought home to him that NATO will defend itself with all means.

7. The main enemy forces offer such tempting targets that they can quickly be annihilated with nuclear means.

8. The morale of the enemy forces and/or the population has sunk so low that a nuclear *coup de grâce* is believed to be all that is required to end the war.

The possible reasons for a switch from conventional to nuclear war are therefore manifold: NATO's own situation may have become so disadvantageous that only nuclear means are considered capable of restoring it (items 2 to 5 above) or the enemy's situation is such that a display of nuclear force would quickly end the war (6 to 8 above). Some of the reasons are purely operational (1, 2, 3, 4 and 7 above) while others involve psychological and morale factors (5, 6 and 8).

When might the enemy consider to switch to nuclear warfare?

We have seen in Chapter 4 that he is more likely to succeed if he chooses battlefield nuclear, in preference to conventional, weapons right from the beginning. But should he start a conventional war, he might subsequently use nuclear weapons for any of the following main reasons:

1. He believes that the defence is about to use nuclear weapons and forestalls it;

2. He is losing battles, his attack has been repelled or his advance halted, and he thinks that only nuclear weapons will enable him to resume the offensive;

3. He needs time for reorganization and thinks he will gain it by switching to nuclear means;

4. He considers the results of interdiction with conventional weapons disappointing and therefore uses nuclear weapons instead;

5. He uses nuclear weapons only against NATO shipping in order to stop oversea reinforcements and supplies from reaching the opposing front;

6. He believes that nuclear weapons will bring about a breakdown in enemy military and/or civilian morale.

The reasons, then, are as varied as those which may prompt the defence to switch to nuclear war.

What can the defender, and the attacker, hope to gain by introducing nuclear weapons, and what disadvantages do they have to face? In the search for an answer to these questions we concern ourselves only with the purely operational reasons which could prompt either side to use nuclear weapons first.

As far as the defence is concerned, it is obvious that it has nothing to lose and much to gain if it forestalls an enemy who is about to initiate nuclear war. It is also obvious that if an attacker concentrates his main forces so strongly that they can be destroyed with atomic weapons and effective resistance be brought to an end, the defence secures only benefits for itself on the battlefield and suffers no disadvantages, on the battlefield, by using them. But in this case the defence must first carefully assess the likely enemy reaction and if it thinks that he will use strategic nuclear weapons in reply, it may well decide to let the opportunity slip and continue the war without resort to battlefield weapons, especially if it has reason to believe that it can win with conventional means.

The problem facing the defence is even more complicated if its losses in men and equipment during the conventional phase have been such that it feels compelled to resort to nuclear weapons. Western commentators agree that if it uses them at all, it must do so at an early stage. Professor Kissinger points out that if the shield forces are allowed to disintegrate it may well be that no additional amount of violence can restore the situation, and battlefield nuclear weapons may then favour the attacker who can keep his units dispersed while the defence must deploy its forces in predictable areas. Professor Kissinger therefore thinks that effective employment of tactical nuclear weapons depends on the strength of the shield forces and 'the optimum, perhaps the only appropriate moment' for the introduction of nuclear weapons is early in the fighting.[1]

Brigadier W. F. K. Thompson holds similar views. A weak conventional defence, he states, 'first encourages the continuation of the (enemy) probe and then introduces nuclear weapons at the most inauspicious moment'.[2] He recommends the early use of nuclear battlefield weapons, not only because this would enable the opponent to reconsider before the tactical air force has been committed, but also because these weapons, if used in

---

[1] 'The Unsolved Problems of European Defense', *Foreign Affairs*, July 1962, Vol. 40, No. 4, pp. 522 and 531.

[2] 'Forgotten Factor in NATO Strategy', *Daily Telegraph* (London), March 5, 1962.

quantity, would produce chaos and stalemate and thus halt the aggression.

Brigadier Thompson also stresses the need to keep a sufficient number of aircraft in reserve so that enough are available for possible nuclear strikes, and so does Mr F. W. Mulley: 'if we indulge in conventional interdiction only, perhaps having to use 100 planes for a job that could be done by two or three armed with nuclear weapons, we might risk losing a big part of our air force, before the need for its nuclear mission was actually reached.'[1]

What emerges from this review is this: The defence must not use up its strength during the conventional phase to such an extent that its nuclear capability would be impaired. The conventional phase must therefore end when the fighting makes its first serious inroads on the nuclear substance of the defence.

What would this mean in practical terms? No figure can be given for what losses in men, weapons and equipment the defence can stand because its own strength and losses must be compared with those of the enemy. In respect of manpower the defence would refuse to accept a change in the ratio of forces to its disadvantage. But we have tried to show that tactical nuclear weapons do not compensate for the lack of troops; nor will the attacker suffer greater losses in manpower than the defence unless his troops are concentrated.

As for weapons and equipment, the moment to switch would have come for the defence when any further losses in its nuclear arsenal—through capture and destruction—would endanger its nuclear effectiveness. And since conventional weapons too are needed in nuclear war, the defence would also have to go over to nuclear fighting if its conventional capability is in danger of becoming insufficient for its role in nuclear war. But again, the NATO forces would gain nothing. 'They must realize that they would immediately be exposed to a Russian riposte in kind and that there is little reason to suppose that they would have acquired any *differential* advantage by shifting the contest up one step from the conventional to the tactical nuclear level'.[2]

The same holds true if the defence were to use tactical nuclear weapons after the loss of territory. The main defensive battle is expected to be fought, within hours or days of the outbreak,

---

[1] 'Europe and the Mediterranean', p. 126.
[2] Strachey, op. cit., p.94.

between the Elbe and the Weser. If the defence were to lose this battle it would be strongly tempted to fire tactical weapons because it probably cannot trade space for time: the opponent can in all likelihood build up his reserves in the early stages of the war more quickly than the defence.

However, it may be possible to obtain some respite by nuclear means if troops, communications and supplies have been dislocated. But there will be a pause only if tactical nuclear weapons are used liberally; an occasional nuclear burst would not compel the enemy to stop and reorganize.

In the bygone days of Imperial Germany the Kaiser used to take part in the autumn manoeuvres as commander of troops. However well or badly the situation had developed for those under his command, at a certain stage he would order his cavalry to charge, and umpires and all others concerned always agreed that by this brilliant move he had won the day, battle and campaign—game, set and match. It was mildly surprising that the opposing general never thought of having his cavalry charge and gain victory.

The first use of tactical nuclear weapons has not the magic effect of the Kaiser's cavalry, the opponent can use the same devices, and he can use them first too. If the defence introduces tactical nuclear weapons, it will have a marginal initial advantage due to surprise, but it does not execute a war-winning manoeuvre. It hopes that while success was denied to it during the conventional phase, nuclear weapons will help to restore the situation. Whether or not these hopes are justified depends on the skill and the means with which it wages nuclear war—and the skill and means of the opponent. In other words, the switch to nuclear war must never be regarded as a remedy *per se*, and with neither side having experience in the use of nuclear weapons, neither should take its superior skill for granted.

We have set out before the disadvantages of transforming a conventional into a limited nuclear war. In the first place, NATO would introduce, and the attacker would reply with, nuclear weapons while the war is fought on NATO territory; they might bring nuclear devastation upon a friendly population and country. The damage might be relatively small, perhaps, to begin with, but looming large is the danger of escalation. Next, if the nuclear remedy is not effective, as it would not be in most cases, no compensating military advantage has been gained. Thirdly, the attacker can more seriously disrupt the sea communications of the defence with nuclear than with conventional weapons, and he will probably benefit more in this respect from the switch than the defence in its attempts to disrupt his land communications. Fourthly, the attacker seems to receive a rather unexpected bonus if one accepts the theories of General Speidel and Captain Liddell Hart: General Speidel tells us that the attacker does not require numerical superiority in nuclear war and Captain Liddell Hart teaches that the attacker does require numerical superiority—and a fairly substantial one—in conventional war. If both authorities are right the attacker can either withdraw troops from the battlefield or extend it and strongly increase his pressure as soon as the war turns nuclear. It seems to us, though, that the attacker will in reality not gain in this way: as the reader will recall, we take the view that near parity of forces is required in conventional war, and the attacker will therefore not be better off, as far as his manpower is concerned, if and when the switch is made.

We can now draw the following conclusions:

NATO should switch to tactical nuclear weapons only in order to forestall the enemy's introduction of nuclear weapons, to reply in kind if he uses them first, and to protect our vital interests when conventional means fail. In the last case NATO cannot expect to gain any lasting military advantage—unless the opponent's troops are concentrated—but nothing must be left untried in such a situation and the opponent may now be willing to reconsider; the time for the switch is not necessarily early in the fighting but when the situation does not permit NATO to wait any longer.

We now turn to the operational reasons which might prompt an attacker to switch to nuclear war. If he is correct in believing that the defence is about to go over to nuclear war, he can only profit if he forestalls it. If he needs time to reorganize he can probably gain it by the liberal use of tactical nuclear weapons. If he initiates nuclear war in order to resume his advance which has been halted by the defence, he might find himself in an unfavourable position in as much as he must concentrate his forces rather more than the defence and if it replies quickly in kind, there might be more chaos in his own ranks than in those of the

[1] Policy Speech before the Economic Club in New York, November 18, 1963.

defence. Here again not the weapon as such but skill and capabilities on both sides will decide the issue.

The general advantages and disadvantages of an attacker who switches to limited nuclear war are apparent: he can more effectively destroy the vital seaports of the West with nuclear than with conventional weapons, and his own population is not immediately affected by a tactical nuclear exchange if he fights on enemy soil, but he must fear the danger of escalation just as much as his opponent.

The one who is more successful on the battlefield has a certain element of choice that the other side lacks: he has a good chance to bring the war to an end before nuclear weapons are used by either side, by offering reasonable peace terms. He might choose this course in order to avoid a nuclear holocaust in his own country, and his opponent, motivated by the same fear may come to terms with him. It is mainly because of this fear that a conventional war may stay conventional throughout and that the switch to a nuclear war may not occur.

PART III

CONCLUSIONS

CHAPTER 8

AN ASSESSMENT OF THE DEBATE

NATO must be able to meet any conventional attack, short of allout aggression, with conventional means because general nuclear war will in all likelihood ensue if NATO replies with tactical nuclear weapons instead, and strategic nuclear weapons are not the answer to a limited conventional attack. For how long a war can be fought conventionally cannot be laid down dogmatically in advance and the reliance on a fixed time limit—of thirty days—seems undesirable because a conventional war may needlessly be turned into a nuclear war, be it by NATO (p. 127) or by its opponent (p. 129). The side that uses tactical nuclear weapons first usually reaps only a limited benefit from the switch and the general disadvantages outweigh as a rule the initial advantages of such an operation.

A war that starts as a conventional war need not stay conventional, and the danger is always present that it may suddenly turn into a nuclear war. Hence three rules follow:

1. The troops fighting a conventional war against a nuclear power must be so deployed as if they were fighting a nuclear war, that is they must be dispersed over a greatly extended battlefield. Otherwise they would in all likelihood make it impossible for their own side to introduce nuclear weapons on the battlefield in the course of the fighting, and they would be exposed to nuclear extinction if the opponent chooses to switch to nuclear war.

2. The conventional war against a nuclear power is characterized by purely mobile operations; there is no fixed front line, no static defence system, no defence zone; the fire-power of both sides will be almost equal, and since mobile defence must be conducted offensively, the defence is nearly as exposed as the attacker. As a result the attacker no longer requires a sizeable numerical superiority, and since the defence must attack and counter-attack almost as much as the attacker, it needs almost as many troops as he does.

3. The weight of the attack would be very much reduced and

possibly be insufficient if the attacker would not deploy part of his forces in the enemy rear, and this is what Soviet doctrine envisages; it foresees frequent air movements of troops to the opponent's rear. A dispersed defence, on the other hand, could not withstand a concentrated attack with conventional means unless it forms concentrations itself or extends the war into the enemy's rear. The first alternative would be undesirable; the second must be adopted, and the rear forces will attack regardless of whether their own 'front' troops are attacking or on the defensive. The role of these rear forces will be to pull back the enemy front by isolating the battlefield and co-operating with their front troops in the single or double envelopment of the enemy. Only by fighting the enemy at his front and in his rear in this manner is it possible to obtain local superiority without forming concentrations and to confront an enemy with strength in dispersal. To make this concept of concentric dispersion effective, the mind of the soldier must be attuned by special training to the peculiar conditions of rear warfare. The troops will move overland into the enemy rear.

Successful rear attacks are also important morale boosters for troops who have hitherto been fighting only defensively. This was precisely the effect of the First Chindit Expedition: by showing that the Japanese enemy could be defeated in jungle fighting, the Chindits restored the confidence of the Army in India in itself—and of Indian civilians in the British.[1]

The concept of concentric dispersion has, perhaps, another merit in the NATO context; it gives a new interpretation to the doctrine of forward defence and brings the official NATO and the German views on its implication more closely together. In NATO's concept forward defence does not mean that the main defence effort will be made right at the Iron Curtain while the Germans have the understandable desire to contain an attacker as near to the frontier as possible. By invading the attacker's rear after battle has commenced, the rear troops engage the enemy in strength close to the frontier without disturbing the deployment of the main defence forces on ground of NATO's choosing further away from the Iron Curtain.

Rear warfare will also be conducted by other than the

[1] Cf. Sykes, *Orde Wingate*, p. 437.

regular troops of either side. An attacker will mobilize his partisans in NATO countries, firstly in order to weaken their resolve to put up a determined fight, and secondly in order to support his troops in the field. This support can be given in various ways: by participating in combat, preparing landing grounds for his airborne troops, assisting in river crossings, sabotaging, harassing, raiding, carrying out reconnaissance and supplying Intelligence. The defence will use partisans for similar purposes, and the American Special Force will always and the British SAS on occasions co-operate with them. Both Special Force and SAS will also attack special targets and the SAS will carry out independent harassing missions, sabotage, ambushing, kidnapping, reconnaissance and generally create alarm and despondency. Similar tasks will be performed for the other side by the East German Reconnaissance Troops which will operate in Bundeswehr uniform.

Finally, there will be airborne operations in the enemy rear. They play a much greater role in the Soviet than in the Western concept. They seem worth while in the future only in Commando operations, Chindit-type operations designed to contain the enemy, and operations for the seizure of strategic positions at the beginning of a war.

Dispersed troops engaged in mobile conventional warfare will not be expected to hold ground; their task is to control it in the way guerrilla forces do. A tactical aim will be to keep the enemy's troops dispersed, the operational aim, as it has always been, to capture or destroy the enemy and win the battle; but moderation must be shown on the strategic level in the exploitation of victory lest the enemy sees himself forced to introduce nuclear weapons.

Obviously, not all national contingents of NATO are of the same high standard or up to the required strength. As a result some frontages are too long. The weakest front will be sought out by the enemy for his main attack. More and better conventional equipment is required. That the best equipped forces, the US 7th Army, are assigned to the comparatively safe region of South Germany is one drawback of the present NATO deployment; that there are so many national 'seams' in the north is another and perhaps more serious one. In the last war it was very often the seam between formations of different nationalities —German, Italian, Hungarian and Rumanian—which the Red

Army selected for its breakthrough attempts and where it was frequently successful.[1]

The logistical support requires improvements, but above all there is a need for larger reserves of greater combat readiness. The Soviet strength, whatever the number of their forces in the European border areas may be, lies in the quick build-up capability of reserves, and it is primarily in this respect that the East is superior to the West. It is here that the greatest effort is required if a conventional conflict is to be kept conventional. Since the defence must be numerically almost as strong as the attacker, the 35 NATO divisions which would be available within a month of an outbreak, plus the territorial defence forces, would not be able to fight conventionally against, say, 40 or 45 of the 65 Soviet and 15 of the 60 satellite divisions available within that same period, and although such a war could not be classified as an all-out war, NATO could not offer prolonged conventional resistance; the war would become nuclear soon after its outbreak. NATO can avoid this danger only by having more combat-ready reserves more quickly available.

The conventional defence doctrines require a larger measure of acceptance than is at present obtained. There is as yet no general agreement on the feasibility of a conventional strategy or the duration of a conventional war or the conventional phase of a war, nor is it realized that the defence must be numerically almost as strong as the attacker if it wants to fight a purely mobile war on the modern battlefield.

The late John Strachey has put the blame for our conventional shortcomings on the failure of doctrine. He thought that the NATO governments have never appreciated what is the true function of their ground forces in Europe. By talking of providing a trip wire or of psychological reassurance they have expressed the belief that only thermonuclear weapons mattered, but they have never faced the military necessities of the era of nuclear parity and still think as if the West had kept its predominance. They have accepted, he went on, that the West could not match the alleged numerical superiority of the East and ignored that Western Europe has more inhabitants than Soviet Russia. 'No doubt', he concluded, 'they have talked like this partly because of the pain and expense of providing

---

[1] A convincing case for the redeployment of NATO forces is made out by Captain Liddell Hart, 'The Defence of West Germany and the Baltic', op. cit., 18 f.

adequate ground forces adequately equipped; but it has also been because of a failure to think out what is the *function* of those ground forces.'[1] Likewise, the West is still inclined to think that tactical nuclear weapons compensate for the lack of divisions although this is no longer so since the East has now also acquired tactical nuclear weapons.

There is no doubt a lot of truth in this argument, and one of the reasons for these misunderstandings is a failure in communications. On several occasions in the past announcements of great significance have been made in America without sufficient prior reference to the European members of the Alliance. More important still, the United States has an obvious self-interest in raising the nuclear threshold because in doing so she minimizes to some extent the danger of escalation and war damage to the home land. The European countries have the same self-interest but, as has often been explained, they are not as clearly aware of it because those in the front line will face great destruction anyway, even if a war remains conventional; they wish to prevent wholesale devastation, be it nuclear *or* conventional, and they consider NATO's resolve to reply to any attack with nuclear weapons as the best means of discouraging a would-be attacker. This is one reason for the lack of European enthusiasm for the American insistence on increasing NATO's conventional strength. The second is that they believe they detect in this insistence a weakening of the American resolve to defend them with nuclear weapons. There are, in addition, impediments of a political nature which account for the reluctance of some European members to give their active support to the upgrading of conventional warfare in NATO doctrine.

If the present East-West détente is more than a passing phase brought about by the Soviet-Chinese dispute, NATO has time to adjust its differences. It has time to evolve an agreed conventional doctrine, but agreement must be obtained, not only in order to conduct a war effectively but also because NATO could otherwise be manoeuvred into a position in which the Alliance might be disrupted.

To initiate the search for such a doctrine and to make a contribution towards its formulation was the purpose of the present study.

[1] Strachey, op. cit., pp. 92–93.

APPENDIX

OPERATIONS
of the
23RD BRITISH INFANTRY BRIGADE
NAGA HILLS
April—July 1944[1]

1. *Introductory*

The following narrative of events . . . is not in any way a comprehensive account of every incident . . . Sketch Map I indicates the general course followed by the operations.

The Bde commenced to move from Central India into ASSAM at the end of March 44 . . . While the columns were in this way crossing India by train, the Japanese advance on KOHIMA and the threat to DIMAPUR and the ASSAM railway had developed to such an extent that the Bde was deflected for operations in that area.

2. *Phase 'A'—Defence of the ASSAM Railway Line*
(a) *Troops available.* The first task allotted to the Bde on arrival at MARIANI was the defence of the railway line from JAMULGIRI to NAZIRA . . .

3. *Phase 'B'—The approach march*
(a) *Initiation of the Plan.* By this date[2] higher comd had agreed that the Bde should more properly be used offensively in an operation of penetration with the object of cutting the communications of the Japanese 31 DIV then besieging KOHIMA. We were allotted the area

---

[1] In the last war there was only one formation of brigade strength which successfully operated for an extended period as *short*-range penetration force in the enemy rear, and that was 23rd British Infantry Brigade. Its tasks were to pull back the enemy front and also to protect the left flank of 33 Corps in its subsequent advance. The brigade had first been assigned to operate in Burma as a long-range penetration group deep in the Japanese rear as part of General Wingate's 'Special Force', better known as Chindits, but it was never employed in that role. It was decided instead to use it in the battle for Assam and it operated there, in the Naga Hills, as ordinary infantry at short range from April to July, 1944.

The main components of 23rd British Infantry Brigade were the 2nd Battalion of the Duke of Wellington's Regiment, the 4th Battalion of the Border Regiment, and the 1st Battalion of the Essex Regiment. They operated in columns, numbered 33, 34, 44, 55, 56, 60, 76 and 88. The Report on Operations of which a shortened version is given above, was written by the commander, Brigadier Lancelot E. C. M. Perowne, in September 1944.

[2] At about the middle of April 1944.

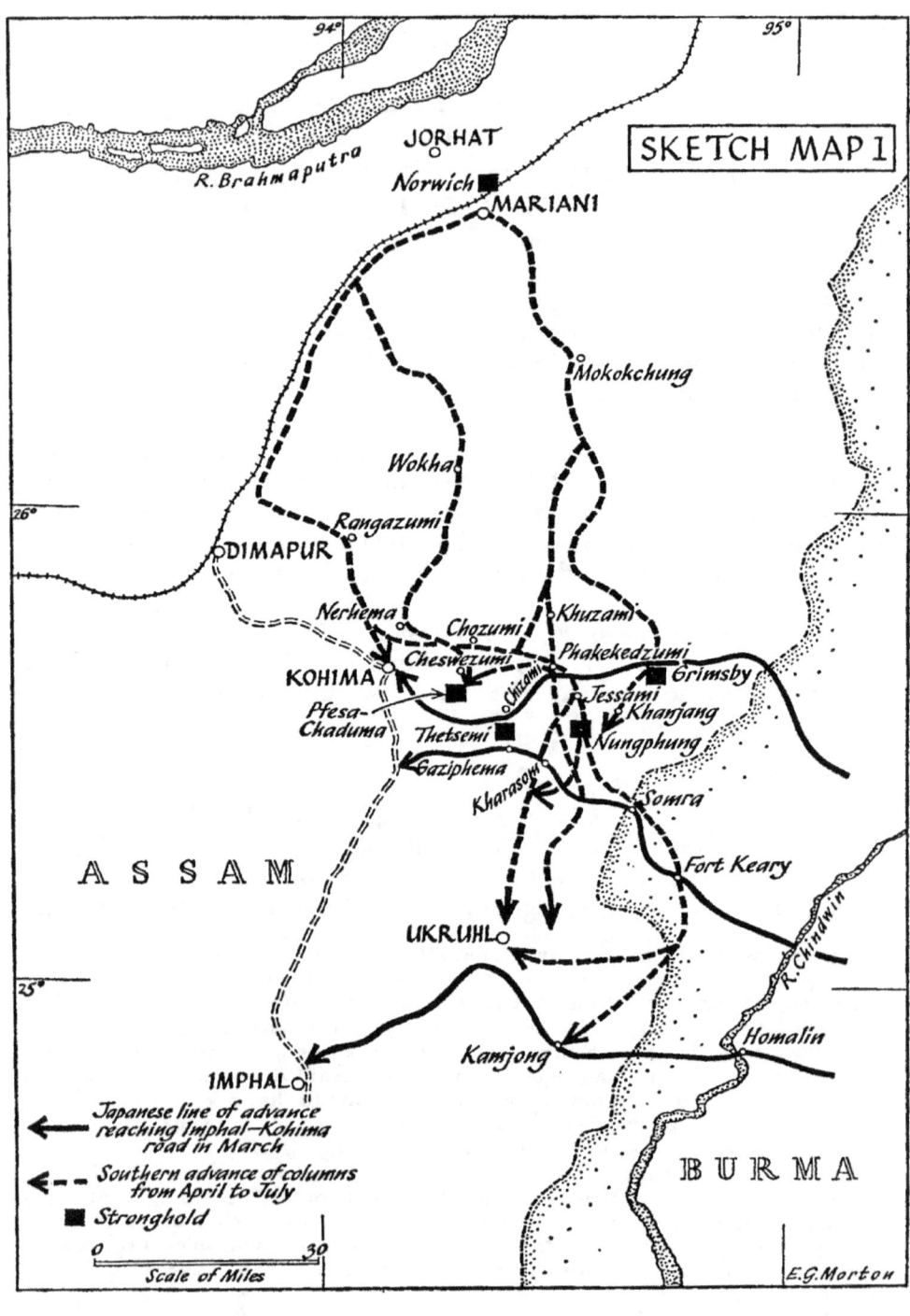

APPENDIX

JESSAMI—KHARASOM—GAZIPHEMA, as a 'target triangle' in which to create the maximum disruption of enemy coming from East, South East, and South. The general plan for advance was that two columns should move down each of the three routes southwards from the RANGAZUMI—MOKOKCHUNG lines until they reached the line of the KOHIMA—JESSAMI track, which was at that time the Japanese main line of communication. On arriving there the columns were to be concentrated in a south-easterly direction and prevent any enemy movement over any of the tracks in the target triangle. The seventh and eighth columns (76 and 88) were then ordered to make a wide flank march east of the TIZU to fall upon JESSAMI and KHANJANG by surprise from the north-east. This plan was to some extent compromised by the initial piecemeal deployment of the Bde, and had to be developed from the not altogether suitable locations and distribution of columns at the close of the Railway Defence Phase.

Thus the two Essex colns shortly became too closely involved in the battle of KOHIMA, and both they and the Duke of Wellington's colns were too near the hub of the wheel for satisfactory employment in a truly marauding role on the Japanese L of C. The Appreciation called for a group of four colns to make the Eastern flank march, and four to make the more direct approach to the target triangle. In the event, two only could be made available for the flank operation and two colns had to do the work of four on the N face of the triangle.

Thus ended the period of static defence of the railway which was gratefully handed over to 33 Bde on the 20th. By the 22nd the last column had set off up into the hills and on the 29th Bde H.Q. moved forward to MOKOKCHUNG. By the end of April therefore, the whole Bde was committed to the hills and moved forward as fast as the terrain and the enemy would permit. On the right the ESSEX columns were directed on KOHIMA; the DUKE OF WELLINGTON'S REGT moved from WOKHA southwards to NERHEMA and the BORDER REGT from MOKOKCHUNG towards PHAKEKEDZUMI. The Gunner columns were following them down from MOKOKCHUNG prior to driving off to the east, on a route to be selected after recce.

(b) *Terrain, Climate and Inhabitants.* The country to be crossed by the colns during their approach marches comprised a tumbled mass of jungle-covered hills rising sheer out of the Plains to an average height of 4,000–6,000 ft . . .

The hills are extremely steep-sided and the jungle covers them thick. All normal movement is therefore confined to the few Govern-

APPENDIX

ment graded bridle paths and the NAGA tracks connecting their villages. These latter lie invariably on the summit of the hills ... The going on these tracks, arduous enough at all times, became extremely treacherous in the rains, when the clay surface was turned into a slippery mass on which neither man nor beast could remain upright ...

(a) *Lines of Communication.* One of the essential differences between this operation and that for which we had prepared was that, whereas we had trained to rely upon the air entirely for supply and the evacuation of casualties and prisoners, we found ourselves here in country largely unsuitable for airstrip construction but provided with tracks which could be made use of to keep touch with rear services in the plains. The development and subsequent maintenance and protection of these tenuous lines of communication became later a very complicated and difficult matter ... Four NAGA PIONEER COYS were raised by us under the direction of my S.O.R.E. and put to work on those tracks ...

A large number of NAGAS were armed with rifles and shotguns and assisted considerably in escort duties and protection of the tracks, and there were only two recorded cases of vehicles being attacked by the enemy.

In spite of all this organization the ground L of C was never entirely satisfactory owing to the nature of the country and was a constant source of anxiety.

(d) *Other special measures found necessary* ...

(e) *Progress of the Approach.* The columns pushed southwards on their allotted courses encountering minor enemy resistance only until reaching the line KOHIMA—PHAKEKEDZUMI. On the right the ESSEX column fought their way through CHESWEMA and THEZAMI and came to rest on the fringe of the Kohima battle. The DUKES arrived at NERHEMA and these four columns were retained for some time by Corps to observe the result of the assault on KOHIMA and were ordered to prevent enemy infiltration northwards while patrolling in order to ascertain the enemy's right flank dispositions. It followed from this that the eastward swing of the line was thrown out of gear and the BORDER columns were obliged to take on a very much bigger area than originally planned.

55 Column came up against resistance at SATHAZUMI and, after a period of patrols and D.A.S., drove the enemy from this place on the 20th of May. The column pursued and again came up against stiff

APPENDIX

resistance at CHESWEZUMI which place they proceeded to contain and harass with mortar, M.M.G. and D.A.S.

34 Column meanwhile pushed rapidly forward as far as KHUZAMI on the main bridle track towards PHAKEKEDZUMI. From here they put in a night raid on PHAKEKEDZUMI on the 1st/2nd May and killed and wounded 42 enemy for 7 casualties of their own. After this event the enemy strongly reinforced PHAKEKEDZUMI and, with a view to getting into position in the target triangle already referred to, 34 Column sidestepped to KHOMI with the object of avoiding PHAKEKEDZUMI, at the same time isolating it from the West and South as the Gunners were doing from the East and South East . . . On the 17th May 60 and 88 Columns fell upon the Japanese establishments at JESSAMI and KHANJANG with complete surprise and success, killing many and taking prisoners as well as some 300 porter loads of material and documents.

By the same date 34 Column had established ambushes on the JESSAMI—KOHIMA road west of CHIZAMI. 55 Column was still occupied with CHOZUMI. Authority had been received from Corps for the DUKES to commence their south-east movement and this had now begun. The ESSEX columns were however still retained off KOHIMA . . .

The South East movement of the DUKES proceeded with extreme deliberation. 76 Column took over from 56 before CHOZUMI on the 19th and 20th and commenced a series of attacks resulting in the enemy being driven out of that place by the 26th. Meanwhile 76 Column pushed across the CHOZUMI track and took up a position at PFESA-CHADUMA from which they based successful minor ambushes on their allotted section of the JESSAMI track. They were at that time in close proximity to 31st Japanese Divisional Headquarters but an attempt to stage a raid was abortive. The enemy countered by attacking the stronghold on the 30th of May, and succeeded in inflicting a few casualties on our column and rendering the place untenable. The column withdrew under cover of dark to reorganize and re-took their position on the following day and were not again molested there.

55 Column being released from before CHOZUMI moved to KHOMI and there took over from 34 Column the task of interrupting traffic on the JESSAMI track between PHAKEKEDZUMI and CHIZAMI. This in turn liberated 34 Column to push forward into the target triangle and by the 31st May the whole column was in stronghold at THETSIMI with ambushes and blocks on the various tracks and in a position to patrol as far as GAZIPHEMA.

APPENDIX

On the extreme left the Gunner columns settled themselves into a stronghold at NUNGPHUNG and, still containing the enemy south of JESSAMI, put out patrols and ambushes on the tracks eastward of KHARASOM. At the same time they despatched a patrol over the MOLHE pass which returned via SOMRA, having displayed itself conspicuously to create the impression of large numbers operating in that area.

(f) *Problem of getting animals forward* . . . It now became necessary to get the animals forward to their columns in order to retain the necessary mobility for further operations in the target triangle and to enable mortars and machine-guns to be taken out of the stronghold by raiding parties. The only route practicable lay through PHAKEKEDZUMI which, as has been explained, was still in Japanese hands.

. . . Patrolling towards PHAKEKEDZUMI was immediately put in hand by the Bde Defence Coy and revealed strong defences there. The task of reducing PHAKEKEDZUMI was given to 55 Column with Bde H.Q. Defence Coy under command. At the same time 'Corps allotted two 3·7 'Hows' in pack and these set off from MARIANI to join Bde H.Q. Column.

The attack on PHAKEKEDZUMI developed over the first five days of June and, after the usual probing attacks with air support and continued harassing by mortars and machine-guns, the enemy were successfully driven from his two outlying covering positions on the 'pimple' and the 'ridge' and on the 5th of June the village was occupied by us . . . 55 Column set off to join 34 at THETSIMI.

(g) *Conclusion of the Approach.* Meanwhile 33 and 76 Columns continued successfully to interrupt communications and destroy parties of Japs in their area. CHESWEZUMI was taken on the 4th and THENIZUMI on the 5th of June, each engagement resulting in enemy casualties without loss to our own columns.

The phase of the approach march was at an end. By the 10th of June therefore, the JESSAMI-KOHIMA L of C had been completely and finally interrupted and six of our columns were operating in the target triangle. The two Essex Columns still remained shackled to KOHIMA where they suffered considerably from disease . . .

(h) *Stronghold at PHAKEKEDZUMI* . . . 33 Corps were meeting with stubborn resistance at KOHIMA but steadily progressing and driving the enemy out of that place. Intelligence received during this

APPENDIX

period suggested a possible counter-offensive by the enemy to reopen his lines of communication and establish himself in positions in the area PHAKEKEDZUMI-JESSAMI. From here he would be able to threaten KOHIMA and the IMPHAL road, deflect a considerable portion of the strength of 33 Corps to contain him (thereby reducing the forces available for opening the road to IMPHAL) and be in a position to proceed with his project when the dry weather returned. It was accordingly decided to maintain and develop the Jap defences at PHAKEKEDZUMI with a view to creating there a stronghold which could be held by the Bde and from which the columns could continue to operate while denying that strategic position to the enemy . . .

4. *Phase 'C'—The period of ambushes*
(a) *Incidence and duration*. The period of ambushes merged with that of the approach . . . By the 13th of May the BORDERS had already commenced a series of ambushes on the KOHIMA-JESSAMI track. By the 20th of May practically all traffic on this route had ceased due chiefly to these ambushes and to the destruction of the Japanese establishments at JESSAMI and KHANJANG by Gunners on the 17th and 18th . . .

Up till May 17th there was considerable enemy traffic both ways on the KOHIMA-JESSAMI track. When this was interrupted in the way above described, the enemy developed a link track connecting KOHIMA to the TOPHEMA-GHAZIPHEMA route and it was along this route that he endeavoured to maintain his last resistance at KOHIMA and along which the bulk of the retreat of the Division eventually took place. When KOHIMA was cleared the road used by him was from TOPHEMA to KHARASOM and then south to UKRUHL or east to SOMRA although the latter route was already in process of being evacuated by him. All his stocks, between KHARASOM and SOMRA for example, were cleared westward on to the UKRUHL route and this movement provided some opportunities for interruption by the Gunner column to the East. Finally he was using only the roads directly south from KHARASOM to UKRUHL . . .

(c) *Results and difficulties*. The period of ambushes proved somewhat disappointing and although a considerable number of Japanese were killed and much material captured, this was mostly done by small parties on a large number of occasions . . . Nothing in the least resembling General WINGATE's 'Grand Ambush' could be brought off in the circumstances in which we found ourselves . . . With all these difficulties and misfortunes we nevertheless achieved some small success and our tale of dead Japanese bodies at the end of the 3rd Phase rested at 347.

APPENDIX

5. *Phase 'D'—Pursuit*

(a) *The Plan.* By early June it was apparent that the Japanese would be forced to withdraw from KOHIMA, and the Army Commander ordered the pursuit to be carried on with the utmost vigour and in spite of all risk with the view to accomplishing the complete destruction of the Japanese 31st Division. So far as this Bde was concerned the orders of the Commander were simplicity itself—'All on UKRUHL'. It was early appreciated that the physical difficulties of the pursuit would be great and that forced marching over vile country and in deteriorating weather would be necessary if we were to achieve any further interruption of the enemy's retreat as opposed to a mere hastening of it from behind . . .

Taking these factors into account and assessing the rate of withdrawal of the enemy and the likelihood of his making a stand at UKRUHL, the plan for the fresh phase provided for a direct advance from the GAZIPHEMA-CHAKYANG line towards UKRUHL by four columns, while the remaining four columns commenced a flank march over the barrier mountain range to cut the enemy's lines of communication from UKRUHL to HOMALIN and fall upon his rear. The BORDERS were allotted the route KHARASOM-UKRUHL, the D.W.R. converging from CHAKYANG, and the ESSEX Regt. and Gunner Colns, marching in the order 56, 60, 88, 44 columns, were to proceed with what speed the terrain and weather would allow via THUSOMKHULEN-SOMRA-FORT KEARY to SAIYAPAW to block the eastern and south eastern exits from UKRUHL and be prepared, when they arrived in that area, to act as circumstances should dictate . . .

(b) *Re-grouping and re-fitting.* Permission had been received from Corps on the 5th of June for the removal of the ESSEX Columns from KOHIMA, and in anticipation of the next phase these columns commenced a flank march across the rear of the DUKE OF WELLINGTON'S Regt., moving via KIDZEMATUMA and RANGAZUMI to PHAKEKEDZUMI. . . . 56 Column left PHAKEKEDZUMI on the 12th June followed by 44 on the 15th, 33 on the 17th and 76 on the 18th June. 60 and 88 were of course already away to the East operating around their stronghold at NUNGPHUNG . . .

(f) *Modification of Plan.* The plan had provided for the concentration of the Bde on the North and Eastern sides of UKRUHL by 1st July. In the event two columns were in contact with the Japanese outside UKRUHL on the north by the 27th of June. Two more were within striking distance by the 2nd July but the Eastern Group . . . were still on the 5th held up at SAIYAPAW well out of striking distance to the East. Meanwhile 33, 80 and 89 Brigades had been advancing

APPENDIX

rapidly from the South-west and West, driving the enemy before them, with the result that not only the 31st Japanese Division but also the bulk of the 15th were now in full retreat South and South-east of UKRUHL. . . . 3 Bde arrived at FURING on the 3rd of July and after conference with the Bde Commander it was agreed that the assault on UKRUHL should be carried out by that formation. To assist in this, it was decided to send the D.W.R. columns down to block the Eastern exits from UKRUHL in the neighbourhood of SIRUHI, and I further undertook with 34 and 55 columns and the Bde Defence Coy to patrol to the North-west and West . . .

The general line of the Japanese retreat led them from UKRUHL southwards to KAMJONG and I decided to make one further attempt using the Eastern Group of columns to harass the enemy's retreat along this track . . .

(g) *Concentration and evacuation.* As events turned out the enemy moved too fast for this last plan to have any real success. On the 6th July 33 Bde took over from the BORDERS in front of UKRUHL. By the 10th they had taken that place . . . There ensued a brief period in which all these columns were killing and taking prisoner small numbers of stragglers, but it soon became apparent that the main pursuit of the Japanese by the other Bdes of 33 Corps was likely to be more interfered with than assisted by our Columns remaining in their positions. . . . Accordingly the Corps Comd issued orders for the concentration of the Bde at UKRUHL and for its evacuation for refit . . .

6. *Conclusion.*

For nearly four months the Bde had been in action at once against nature and the enemy without rest or relief. In that time it had contributed to a major defeat of the Japanese Army, and killed, wounded and taken prisoner 854 of them for a total loss to themselves of 74 killed and 88 wounded.

BIBLIOGRAPHY

BOOKS

ALLEN, W. E. D.: 'Gideon Force', in IRWIN R. BLACKER (ed.), *Irregulars, Partisans, Guerrillas*. New York, 1954.
BLACKETT, P. M. S.: *Studies of War, Nuclear and Conventional*. Edinburgh and London, 1962.
BROWN, Neville: *Strategic Mobility*. London and New York, 1963.
BUCHAN, Alastair: *NATO in the 1960's*. London and New York, 1960.
────── and WINDSOR, Philip: *Arms and Stability in Europe*. London and New York, 1963.
BUNDESMINISTERIUM FUER VERTEIDIGUNG: *Heeresflieger*. Die Heftreihe Unser Heer, Heft 3. Hamburg, 1962.
CALVERT, Brigadier Michael: *Prisoners of Hope*. London, 1952.
CRAIG, Gordon A.: 'Germany and NATO: The Rearmament Debate', in Klaus KNORR (ed.): *NATO and American Security*. Princeton, 1959.
DINERSTEIN, H. S.: *War and the Soviet Union: Nuclear Weapons and the Revolution in Soviet Military and Political Thinking*. London and New York, 1959.
DIXON, Brigadier C. A. and HEILBRUNN, Otto: *Communist Guerrilla Warfare*. London and New York, 1954; Paris, 1956; Frankfurt-am-Main, 1956; New Delhi, 1963.
EDMONDS, Brigadier-General James E. (comp.): *History of the Great War, Based on Official Documents: Military Operations, France and Belgium, 1914*. London, 1933.
FALLS, Captain Cyril: *The Nature of Modern Warfare*. London, 1941.
FERGUSSON, Brigadier Sir Bernard: *The Wild Green Earth*. London, 1946.
FRETTER-PICO, General Maximilian: *Missbrauchte Infanterie*. Frankfurt-am-Main, 1957.
FULLER, Major-General J. F. C.: *The Second World War, 1939-45*. London, 1948.
──────: *The Conduct of War, 1789-1961*. London and New Brunswick, N.J., 1961.
GALLOIS, General Pierre: *Stratégie de l'âge nucléaire*. Paris, 1960; New York (*Balance of Terror*), 1961.
GARTHOFF, Raymond L.: *Soviet Strategy in the Nuclear Age*. London, 1958; New York (Revised Edition), 1962.

BIBLIOGRAPHY

———: *The Soviet Image of Future War*. Washington, D.C., 1959.
GAVIN, Lt.-General James M.: *War and Peace in the Space Age*. New York, 1958.
GIAP, General Vo Nguyên: *People's War, People's Army*. New York, 1962.
GOOLD-ADAMS, Richard (Rapporteur): *The British Army in the Nuclear Age*. By an Army League Study Group. London, 1959.
GORDON, Harold J.: *Die Reichswehr und die Weimarer Republik, 1919–1926*. Frankfurt-am-Main, 1956
GREENE, Lt.-Colonel T. N. (ed.): *The Guerrilla—And How to Fight Him*. New York, 1962.
de GUINGAND, Major-General Sir Francis: *Operation Victory*. London, 1947.
HALPERIN, Morton H.: *Limited War in the Nuclear Age*. London and New York, 1963.
HART, Captain B. H. Liddell: *Deterrent or Defence*. London, 1960.
HEILBRUNN, Otto and DIXON, Brigadier C. A.: *Communist Guerrilla Warfare*. London and New York, 1954.
———: *The Soviet Secret Services*. London and New York, 1956. Frankfurt-am-Main, 1956.
———: *Partisan Warfare*. London and New York, 1962; Paris, 1964; Frankfurt-am-Main, 1963.
———: *Warfare in the Enemy's Rear*. London, 1963; New York, 1964.
HILSMAN, Roger: 'Strategic Doctrines for Nuclear War', in KAUFMAN, William W. (ed.): *Military Policy and National Security*. London and Princeton, 1956.
———: 'NATO, The Developing Strategic Context'. In KNORR, Klaus (ed.): *NATO and American Security*. Princeton, 1959.
HOAG, Malcolm W.: 'The Place of Limited War in NATO Strategy'. In KNORR, Klaus (ed.): *NATO and American Security*. Princeton, 1959.
HOWARD, Michael: *Disengagement in Europe*. London and New York, 1958.
HOWELL, Major Edgar M.: *The Soviet Partisan Movement, 1941–44*. Washington, D.C., 1956.
KAHN, Herman: *Thinking About The Unthinkable*. London and New York, 1962.
KAUFMAN, William W.: 'Force and Foreign Policy'. In KAUFMAN, William W. (ed.): *Military Policy and National Security*. London and Princeton, 1956.
KIRBY, Major-General S. Woodburn: *The War Against Japan*, Vol. iii. London and New York, 1961.
KISSINGER, Henry A.: *Nuclear Weapons and Foreign Policy*. New York, 1957.
———: *The Necessity for Choice*. London, 1960; New York, 1961.

BIBLIOGRAPHY

KNORR, Klaus: 'Aspects of NATO Strategy; A Conference Report'. In KNORR, Klaus (ed.): *NATO and American Security*. Princeton, 1959.
——— and READ, Thornton (ed.): *Limited Strategic War*. London and New York, 1962.
MAO TSE-TUNG, *Selected Works*. Vol. II London, 1954.
MELLENTHIN, Major-General F. W. von: *Panzer Battles, 1939–1945*. London, 1955; New York, 1956.
MIKSCHE, Lt.-Colonel F. O.: *Atomic Weapons and Armies*. London, 1955; New York, 1959.
———: *The Failure of Atomic Strategy*. London and New York, 1959.
MONTGOMERY, Field Marshal Viscount: *El Alamein to the River Sangro*. British Army of the Rhine Printing and Stationery Service, 1946.
MULLEY, F. W., MP: *The Politics of Western Defence*. London and New York, 1962.
OSGOOD, Robert Endicott: *Limited War: The Challenge to American Strategy*. Chicago, 1957.
———: *NATO, The Entangling Alliance*. Chicago, 1962.
PARSON, Lt.-Colonel Nels A.: *Missiles and the Revolution in Warfare*. Cambridge, Mass., 1962.
READ, Thornton: 'Limited Strategic War and Tactical Nuclear War'. In KNORR, Klaus, and READ, Thornton (ed.): *Limited Strategic War*. London and New York, 1962.
REICHSARCHIV: *Der Weltkrieg 1914–1918. Die militärischen Operationen zu Lande*. Fünfter Band, Berlin. 1929.
RENTSCH, Hellmuth: *Partisanenkampf, Erfahrungen und Lehren*. Frankfurt-am-Main, 1961.
RIDGWAY, Matthew B.: *The Memoirs of Matthew B. Ridgway*. New York, 1956.
ROYAL INSTITUTE OF INTERNATIONAL AFFAIRS: *On Limiting Atomic War*. London, 1956.
SCHELLING, Thomas C.: *The Strategy of Conflict*. Cambridge, Mass., 1963.
SCHMIDT, Helmut: *Defence or Retaliation*. London and New York, 1962.
SENGER UND ETTERLIN, General M. F. von: *Der Gegenschlag, Kampfbeispiele und Führungsgrundsätze der beweglichen Abwehr*. Neckargemund, 1959.
SLESSOR, Marshal of the RAF Sir John: *Strategy for the West*. London and New York, 1954.
———: *The Great Deterrent*. London, 1957; New York, 1958.
———: *What Price Co-existence?* London, 1962; New York, 1961.
SLIM, Field Marshal Viscount: *Defeat Into Victory*. London, 1956; New York, 1961.

BIBLIOGRAPHY

SOKOLOVSKY, Marshal V. D. (ed.): *Military Strategy: Soviet Doctrine and Concepts*. London and New York, 1963.
STRACHEY, John: *On the Prevention of War*. London, 1962; New York, 1963.
SYKES, Christopher: *Wassmuss, 'The German Lawrence'*. London, 1936.
———: *Orde Wingate*. London and New York, 1959.
THOMPSON, P. A.: *Lions Led by Donkeys*. London, 1927.
TUKER, Lt.-General Sir Francis: *Approach to Battle*. London, 1963·
WEINSTEIN, Major Adelbert: *Keiner kann den Krieg gewinnen*. Bonn, 1955.
WINDSOR, Philip and BUCHAN, Alastair: *Arms and Stability in Europe*. London and New York, 1963.
WYNNE, Captain G. C.: *If Germany Attacks: The Battle in Depth in the West*. London, 1940.

ARTICLES AND LECTURES

BAZ, Colonel I.: 'The Characteristics of Modern War'. *Survival*, November/December 1959, pp. 180 ff. Also under the title 'Soviet Military Science on the Character of Contemporary War' in Raymond L. Garthoff: *The Soviet Image of Future War*. Washington, D.C., 1959, p. 96.
BEUNINGEN, Otl K. von: 'Artillerie Regiment oder Brigade Artillerie'. *Revue Militaire Générale*, July 1960, p. 253 f.
BOYLSTON, Lt.-Colonel William L.: 'Armor on the Atomic Battlefield'. *Armor*, May/June 1957, Vol. LXVI, No. 3, p. 29.
BROWN, Neville: 'The Armies in Central Europe'. *The Royal United Service Institution Journal*, November 1963, Vol. CVIII, No. 632, p. 346.
BUZZARD, Rear Admiral Sir Anthony: 'Limited War Capability'. *The Hawk, The Journal of the Royal Air Force Staff Colleges*, No. 24, December 1962, p. 15.
COWLEY, Lt.-General Sir John G.: 'Future Trends in Warfare'. Lecture reprinted in *The Royal United Service Institution Journal*, February 1960, Vol. CV, No. 617, p. 4.
DEUTSCHER SOLDATENKALENDER 1959: 'Der Kampf und Untergang des Schillschen Korps'. Siebentes Jahrbuch, München-Lochhausen, p. 93.
ENTHOVEN, Alain C.: 'American Deterrent Policy'. Address reprinted in *Survival*, May/June 1963, Vol. 5, No. 3, p. 96.
GALE, General Sir Richard N.: 'The Training of Land Forces'. *Revue Militaire Générale*, December 1959, p. 605.

BIBLIOGRAPHY

———: 'A Critical Appraisal of NATO.' Lecture reprinted in *The Royal United Service Institution Journal*, May 1961, Vol. CVI, No. 622, p. 159.
GROSSE, Generalmajor Dr Walther: 'Aus der Geschichte des deutschen Freikorps'. *Deutscher Soldatenkalender 1959*, Siebentes Jahrbuch. München-Lochhausen, p. 131.
HARRIGAN, Anthony: 'Tanks in Nuclear War, a Russian View'. *Armor*, July/August 1963, p. 40.
HART, Captain B. H. Liddell-: 'Small Atomics—A Big Problem'. *Marine Corps Gazette*, December 1959, Vol. 43, No. 12, p. 12.
———: 'Guerrilla War: Factors and Reflections'. *Marine Corps Gazette*, December 1962, Vol. 46, No. 12, p. 22.
———: 'The Defence of West Germany and the Baltic'. *Marine Corps Gazette*, February 1964, Vol. 48, No. 2, p. 18 f.
HEALEY, Denis, MP: House of Commons Debate, March 1, 1955. *Hansard*, col. 1935.
HEILBRUNN, Otto: 'Soviet Military Strategy'. *The Royal United Service Institution Journal*, August 1963, Vol. CVIII, No. 631, p. 270.
HOWZE, Major-General Hamilton H.: 'The Land Battle in an Atomic War'. *Army*, July 1961, Vol. 11, No. 12, p. 32.
———: Report on Battlefield Air-Transport. *Army, Navy and Air Force Journal and Register*, Sept. 29, 1962.
JONES, Lt.-Colonel Alun Gwynne: 'Modern Strategic Concepts'. Lecture reprinted in *The Royal United Service Institution Journal*, February 1963, Vol. CVIII, No. 629, p. 9.
———: 'Army Communications to be Reorganized'. *The Times* (London), September 7, 1962.
———: 'Training for Non-Nuclear Warfare'. *The Times* (London), May 6, 1963.
———: 'Lack of Infantry the Crucial Weakness'. *The Times* (London), October 17, 1963.
KING, James E. Jr: 'Nuclear Plenty and Limited War'. *Foreign Affairs*, January 1957, Vol. 35, No. 2, p. 245.
KISSINGER, Professor Henry A.: 'The Unsolved Problems of European Defense'. *Foreign Affairs*, July 1962, Vol. 40, No. 4, p. 522
LEMNITZER, General L. L.: Interview with Dr Tom Margerison. *The Sunday Times* (London), October 6, 1963.
LEONOV, Lt.-Colonel K.: 'Logistics and Supply of the Soviet Army'. First printed in *Military Review* and reprinted in *Canadian Army Journal*, July 1959, Vol. xiii, No. 3, p. 110.
LIELL, Captain William J.: 'Soviet Airborne'. *Journal of the United Service Institution of India*, October/December 1962, p. 319.

BIBLIOGRAPHY

McCOLL, Captain Alexander M. S.: 'Should Logistics Go Tactical in Nuclear War?' *Armor*, January/February 1963, p. 26.

McNAMARA, Robert: Policy Speech of November 18, 1963, before the Economic Club in New York. *The Times* (London), November 19, 1963.

MARGERISON, Dr Tom: Interview with General Lemnitzer. *The Sunday Times* (London), October 6, 1963.

MAURACH, Dr Bruno: 'Die sowjetischen Luftlandetruppen'. *Revue Militaire Générale*, October 1962, p. 373.

MELLENTHIN, Major-General F. W. von: 'Armor in the Atomic Age'. *Ordnance*, July/August 1960, reprinted in *Canadian Army Journal*, Summer 1960, Vol. xiv, No. 3, p. 55.

MESSMER, Pierre: 'Notre politique militaire'. *Revue de Défense Nationale*, May 1963, p. 751.

MONTGOMERY, Field Marshal Viscount: 'The Panorama of Warfare in a Nuclear Age'. Lecture reprinted in *The Royal United Service Institution Journal*, November 1956, Vol. CI, No. 604, p. 506.

———: 'The Present State of the Game in the Contest Between East and West, and the Future Outlook'. Lecture reprinted in *The Royal United Service Institution Journal*, November 1958, Vol. CIII, No. 612, p. 479.

MULLEY, F. W., MP: 'Europe and the Mediterranean'. Lecture reprinted in *The Royal United Service Institution Journal*, May 1963, Vol. CVIII, No. 630, p. 125.

NOIRET, General Jean: 'Les formes de la guerre et de l'Armée future'. *Revue de Défense Nationale*, January 1963, p. 12.

OGORKIEWICZ, Richard M.: 'Missiles Against Armor'. *Marine Corps Gazette*, January 1959, No. 1, Vol. 43, p. 55.

PICKERT, General W.: 'Vom Wert der zahlenmässigen Stärke im Atomzeitalter'. *Revue Militaire Générale*, February 1961, p. 200; and under the title 'The Value of Numbers in the Nuclear Age' in *Survival*, September/October 1961, Vol. 3, No. 5, p. 229.

POPE, Major W. H.: 'Problems of Future War: The tactical Doctrine and Organization Required by Land Forces'. *Canadian Army Journal*, April 1959, Vol. xiii, No. 2, p. 49.

QUINN, Lt.-Colonel J. T.: 'Some New Aids to Intelligence'. *Australian Army Journal*, July 1963, No. 170, p. 39.

ROMULUS: 'Future Employment of Airborne Forces'. *The Royal United Service Institution Journal*, May 1955, Vol. C, No. 598, p. 239.

SCHULER, Oberst Emil: 'Zusammenarbeit französischer Streitkräfte mit deutschen territorialen Dienststellen'. *Revue Militaire Générale*, December 1962, p. 644.

———: 'Die Landesverteidigung in der Bundesrepublik'. *Revue Militaire Générale*, March 1963.

BIBLIOGRAPHY

SHACKLETON, Major N. A.: 'Anti-Tank Weapons and their Influence in Battle'. *Canadian Army Journal*, Summer 1961, Vol. xv, No. 3, p. 38.

SHTEMENKO, Colonel General: 'Combat Training of Ground Troops for Modern War'. *Survival*, July/August 1963, Vol. 5, No. 4, p. 181; and *Army*, March 1963, p. 47.

SLESSOR, Marshal of the RAF Sir John: 'Britain and the Threshold'. *Daily Telegraph* (London), September 7, 1962.

SMALLMAN, Colonel W. A.: 'Mobility and Logistics'. *Revue Militaire Générale*, March 1960, p. 295.

SPEIDEL, General Dr Hans: 'Mission and Needs of NATO's Shield'. *Army*, September 1960, Vol. 11, No. 2, p. 34.

THOMPSON, Brigadier W. F. K.: 'Revolution on the Battlefield'. *Daily Telegraph* (London), March 8, 1960, and *Survival*, May/June 1960, Vol. 2, No. 3, p. 113.

———: 'Forgotten Factor in NATO Strategy'. *Daily Telegraph* (London), March 5, 1962.

WINGATE, Major-General Orde: 'Special Force Commander's Training Note No. 8—The Stronghold.' Issued February 27, 1944. Reprinted in Brigadier Michael Calvert: *Prisoners of Hope*, p. 274.

———: 'Training Notes' (no date or number). Reprinted in Otto Heilbrunn, *Warfare in the Enemy's Rear*, p. 210.

INDEX

Airborne forces, 31, 34 f., 41, 46, 49, 53, 54, 92, 102, 103, 104, 112, 114, 115, 120
Air force, 32, 34, 46, 50, 53, 54, 74, 75, 76, 106, 109 f., 132
Air reconnaissance, 50
Alam Halfa, 66, 72
Allen, W. E. D., 96
Anti-tank weapons, 55, 56, 69, 70, 76, 117, 118
Armoured forces, 32, 35, 41, 42, 51, 53, 54, 55, 67, 73, 114, 116 f., 127
Armoured personnel carriers, 67, 73, 78, 81, 117, 118
Artillery, 54, 57, 70, 73, 74, 75, 80, 119
   gun, 41, 55, 122
   rocket, 41, 55, 77, 122
Atomic demolition munitions, 53
Auchinleck, Field Marshal Sir Claude, 92

Bacteriological warfare, 123
Bagramian, Marshal, 40
Baz, Colonel I., 34, 40, 41, 93
Beuningen, Otl. K. von, 74
Blacker, Irwin R., 96
Blackett, Professor P. M. S., 20
Bonin, Oberst, 43
Bose, Subhas Chandra, 110
Boylston, Lt.-Colonel William L., 47
Brandenburg Division, 30, 31, 110
Brown, Neville, 13, 45, 76, 77, 115, 119, 120, 127
Buchan, Alastair, 13, 20, 22, 42, 50, 74
Bundesministerium für Verteidigung, 120
Buzzard, Rear Admiral Sir Anthony, 23, 76, 77

Calvert, Brigadier Michael, 101, 115
Chemical warfare, 123
Chindits, 30, 31, 101, 102, 121, 140
   see also Special Force (Chindits)
Commandos, 30, 31, 102
Communication system, 123
Concentration
   for attack, 19, 38, 39, 41, 44, 52, 53, 54, 68
   for defence, 19, 30, 39, 43, 44, 51, 87
Concentric dispersion, 104, 123, 140
Continuous front, 40, 54, 63 f.
Control of territory, 45, 46, 141
Conventional aggression, 23, 28, 29, 85, 86
Conventional forces
   need for, 11, 22, 23, 24, 139, 142
   Nato goal for, 12
Conventional warfare
   conduct of, 35, 102 f.
   deployment for, 38, 63 f., 102 f.
   duration of, 25, 127, 139, 142
   organization and structure, 114 f.
   scope for, 25, 26, 86, 87
   Soviet view on, 12
   switch to nuclear war, 83, 85, 128, 129 f.
   training for, 124
Cowley, Lt.-General Sir John, 20
Craig, Gordon A., 43

Defence concentrations, see concentrations for defence
Defence, mobile and static, 51, 52, 63 f., 69 f., 78, 87 f.
Defence superiority over attacker, see Superiority, numerical
Defensive localities, 51
Deployment, see Conventional war, deployment for, and Nuclear war, deployment for
Depth of operations, 48
Deterrent, see Nuclear warfare, deterrent
Dinerstein, H. S., 37
Dispersal of troops, 19, 38, 42, 43, 44, 45, 47, 54, 55, 74, 87, 104
Dixon, Brigadier, C. A., 50
Dual purpose weapons, 122

East Germany, 12, 112
Edmonds, Brigadier-General James E., 64

INDEX

El Alamein, 71, 72
Enthoven, Alain C., 23
Escalation, see Nuclear war, escalation

Falkenhayn, General von, 64
Falls, Captain Cyril, 65
Firepower, 38, 49, 74 f., 117
Frederick the Great, 63
Freecorps, 108
Fretter-Pico, General Maximilian, 66
Forward defence strategy, 44, 84, 140
Fuller, Major-General J. F. C., 63, 64, 65, 90

Gale, General Sir Richard, 48, 50, 58, 75, 124
Gallois, Général Pierre, 21
Garthoff, Raymond L., 21, 34, 35, 40, 42, 93
Gavin, Lt.-General James M., 36, 48, 56, 57
Gavrisheff, Major, 113
Gazala, 79
Giap, General Vo Nguyên, 95
Goold-Adams, Richard, 54
Gordon, Harold J., 109
Gothic Line, 65
Greene, Lt.-Colonel T. N., 95
Grosse, General-Major Dr. Walther, 108
Guingand, Major-General Sir Francis, 99

Hackett, Lt.-Gen. Sir John W., 21, 30, 125
Halperin, Morton H., 20
Harrigan, Anthony, 41, 42
Hart, Captain B. H. Liddell, 20, 21, 26, 28, 45, 56, 66, 71, 72, 111, 116, 118, 127, 134, 142
Hassel, U. von, 57
Healey, Denis, 22
Heilbrunn, Otto, 21, 35, 46, 50, 57, 91, 94, 96, 102, 104, 110
Hilsman, Roger, 20, 29, 47, 51
Hoag, Malcolm W., 20
Howard, Professor Michael, 22
Howell, Major Edgar M., 96
Howze, Major-General Hamilton H., 55, 56, 75
Hungary, 12

Inchon landing, 92, 106
Independent companies, 30
Infantry, armoured, 67, 73, 78, 81, 117, 118
Institute for Strategic Studies, 126
Intelligence, 49, 107

Jitra Line, 65
Jones, Lt.-Colonel Alun Gwynne, 20, 22, 27, 53, 76, 118, 123

Kahn, Herman, 18
Kaufman, William W., 20
Kennedy, President John F., 24
King, James E., 38
Kirby, Major-General S. Woodburn, 92, 101
Kissinger, Professor Henry A., 21, 22, 23, 27, 38, 39, 43, 45, 46, 82, 131
Knorr, Klaus, 18, 20, 23, 43

Lemnitzer, General L. L., 84
Leonov, Lt.-Colonel K., 113
Liell, Captain William J., 36
Linear defence, see Continuous front
Logistics, 48, 49, 54, 83, 102, 103, 113, 118, 125 f., 142

MacArthur, General D., 92
McColl, Captain Alexander M. S., 48
McNamara, Robert, 12, 13
Magelov, General, 34
Maginot Line, 65, 97
Manoeuvre, war of, 40, 43, 46, 63, 72
Mao Tse-tung, 94
Marauders, 30, 31
Margerison, Tom, 84
Martin, Harold H., 36
Maurach, Bruno, 34
Mellenthin, Major-General F. W. von, 66, 68, 116
Messmer, Pierre, 57, 111
Miksche, Lt.-Colonel F. O., 20, 21, 22, 37, 38, 42, 43, 44, 49, 55, 57, 89, 122, 127
Militia, see Territorial Force
Mius Line, 65
Model, Field Marshal Walter, 66
Montgomery, Field Marshal Viscount, 21, 58, 72

INDEX

Motorized forces, 32, 35, 41, 54
Mulley, F. W., 22, 25, 29, 38, 132

Nassau Conference, 24
NATO meetings, 11, 25, 26
NATO strength, 12, 13, 74, 142
Noiret, Général d'Armée Jean, 45, 47, 48
Norstad, General, 24
Nuclear warfare
  conduct of, 33 f., 36, 40 f., 50 f.
  deployment for, 38 f., 82, 85 f.
  deterrent, 17, 18, 19, 21, 22, 23, 27, 134
  escalation, 18, 135
  likelihood of, 22, 86 f.
  pause, 26
  reasons for, 17, 129, 130, 134
  structure and organization, 113 f.
  switch to, *see* Conventional warfare, switch to nuclear war
  targets, 41, 42, 44, 51, 52
  training for, 124
  weapons,
    first use of, 17, 19, 22, 26, 85, 129 f.
    tactical, 18, 19, 20, 26, 44, 86, 129 f., 143

Organization and structure, 114 f.
Osgood, Robert E., 18, 21, 22, 26
Osorkievicz, Richard M., 116
Ottawa, 11, 25

Parson, Lt.-Colonel Nels A., 36, 53, 57, 121
Partisans, 32, 45, 49, 50, 91, 93, 94 f., 102, 107, 110, 112, 141
Partisan warfare, German aptitude for, 107 f.
Pentomic division, 114, 127
Perowne, Major-General L. E. C. M., 145 f.
Pickert, General, 20, 47
Pokrovsky, Major-General, 34
Poland, 12
Pope, Major W. H., 113, 118, 120

Quinn, Lt.-Colonel J. T., 49

Rangers, 30, 31, 102
Read, Thornton, 18, 38, 39

Rear warfare
  Soviet doctrine, 33 f., 140
  western doctrines, 32 f., 88, 89 f., 140
  in World War II, 30 f., 45, 50, 91, 94 f.
  in Indo-China, 95
  in our own rear, 111
Rentsch, Hellmuth, 107
Ridgway, General Matthew B., 36
ROAD division, 115, 117
Rommel, Field Marshal E., 66, 67, 72, 79
Rotmistrov, Marshal, 40, 41, 42
Royal Institute of International Affairs, 18
Rudakov, Major-General, 34

SAS, 30, 46, 93, 102
Schelling, Thomas C., 76
Schill, Major von, 108
Schmidt, Helmut, 20, 22, 29, 43
Schuler, Oberst Emil, 57, 111
Senger und Etterlin, General M. F. von, 67, 68
Shackleton, Major N. A., 117
Shtemenko, Colonel-General, 41, 47, 50
Siegfried Line, 65
Skorzeny's Special Formation, 30, 31, 110
Slessor, Marshal of the RAF, Sir John, 21, 56, 57, 83
Slim, Field Marshal Viscount, 54, 101, 124
Smallman, Colonel W. A., 126
Sokolovsky, Marshal V. D., 35, 40, 42, 46, 47, 57, 77, 120
Soviet doctrine, 12, 17, 33 f., 40 f., 46, 57, 93, 112
Soviet strength, 12, 13, 127, 142
Special Force (Chindits), 91, 99 f.
Special Force (U.S.), 46, 94, 102, 110, 141
Special Forces, 30, 31, 46, 50, 93, 102, 103, 107
Special Service Force, 30
Speidel, General Dr. Hans, 81, 134
Stay-behind parties, 83
Strachey, John, 17, 22, 24, 121, 132, 143
Structure and organization, 114 f.
Superiority, numerical, 47, 51, 65, 69 f.
Supplies, 25, 48, 49, 70, 83, 102, 113, 118, 125 f.

INDEX

Sykes, Christopher, 47, 92, 101, 109, 110, 140

Tactical Nuclear Weapons, *see* Nuclear Warfare, weapons, tactical
Talensky, Major-General, 40, 48
Target acquisition, 50, 54
Territorial Force, 56, 87, 111
Thompson, P. A., 65
Thompson, Brigadier W. F. K., 37, 80, 131
Thorneycroft, Peter, 18
Tito, Marshal, 94, 99
Tobruk, 71, 79
Training, 124
Truong Chinh, 91
Tuker, Lt.-General Sir Francis, 79

Warsaw Pact, 12, 13, 127
Wassmuss, Consul, 109, 110
Weinstein, Major Adelbert, 43
Western European Union, 24
William II, Emperor, 133
Windsor, Philip, 13, 50, 74
Wingate, Major-General Orde, 31, 47, 91 f., 95, 99 f.
Winter Line, 65
Wynne, Captain G. C., 65, 71

For Product Safety Concerns and Information please contact our EU
representative GPSR@taylorandfrancis.com
Taylor & Francis Verlag GmbH, Kaufingerstraße 24, 80331 München, Germany

www.ingramcontent.com/pod-product-compliance
Lightning Source LLC
Chambersburg PA
CBHW052128300426
44116CB00010B/1821